AIRBORNE FOR THE DURATION

Eric Barfoot DFC

AIRBORNE FOR THE DURATION

The Odyssey of the Ruptured Crab

Warrant Officer Eric Barfoot DFC (RAF Retired)

(Formerly of 37, 70, 216 and 267 Squadrons)

The Book Guild Ltd
Sussex, England

First published in Great Britain in 2004 by
The Book Guild Ltd
25 High Street
Lewes, East Sussex
BN7 2LU

Typesetting in Times by
SetSystems Ltd, Saffron Walden, Essex

Printed in Great Britain by
CPI Bath

A catalogue record for this book is
available from the British Library

ISBN 1 85776 856 6

THE SWANSONG OF THE SERGEANT PILOT

*Fifty years on and fifty years late, this is the
story of the airmen pilots and aircrew.
Most famous and infamous leaders of high
rank were deemed to have won or lost this
or that battle or campaign. They have all
been written about elsewhere. Here an effort
has been made to show what sort of help they
were given, by those they manoeuvred and led.*

CONTENTS

AND SO TO WAR

'Remember, remember the fifth of November, gunpowder, treason and plot.' This date in 1941 would certainly not be forgotten. This was what eight months of flying training had all been about, and now, briefing over, it was next stop Gib.

The night was cold and raw with bursts of threatening rain on a gusty wind. Subdued, we stepped out onto the tarmac of our aircraft dispersal at Hampstead Norris after pensively riding the few miles from Harwell. One by one the paraffin goose-necks flared and fluttered in the wind, as the airmen of the watch marked out the line of take-off. The dim lights of the taxying tracks reflected our mood. The Wingco exchanged a few words with our observer and with the NCO in charge of the ground crew. A short, chubby WAAF corporal cook, a Welsh lass, gave us each a packet of sandwiches, a bar of chocolate, an orange and a very wet kiss. Tears were streaming down her face. None of us knew her, but she made us feel like knights of old off on a crusade. We knew we would be in her prayers until she heard of our safe arrival, and until the departure of the next crew.

The late night take-off was my first with this new crew. The skipper was very experienced having been a long-serving flight commander with a Wapiti squadron on the North West Frontier. I was anxious to be accepted.

One at a time we climbed up the short ladder into the

bomb aimer's position and made our way to our stations. Checks were made and duties assumed automatically. Engines were started, chocks were removed and *'ell for Leather* lumbered to the runway. With engines 'run up' and cockpit checks completed, she turned into wind. Given a green Aldis signal, Wingco wound up the engines on his brakes. I had the less onerous task of holding the throttles against the stops. Suddenly off came the brakes and the Wimp lurched forward, gathering speed, curtseying heavily over the undulating hilltop runway. Long before the perimeter she launched and wallowed into the clearing sky. Training was behind us – this was for real.

The flight from Hampstead Norris to Gibraltar took far longer than any previous ones. Eight hours and fifty-five minutes; four hours of this at night. It was very turbulent whilst we tried to keep just under broken cloud cover, well to the west of Brest and across the Bay of Biscay. Though interception was unlikely, no-one relaxed. The coast of neutral Portugal was followed at a wary distance and, by the time the flight was over, we were a team. The skipper seemed satisfied with my instrument flying, and he made me do most of it. We had no automatic pilot.

How my life had changed in just a week! On 29th October the Flight Commander at the Operational Training Unit had informed me that a co-pilot on the course ahead had become unfit. Since my crew were the nearest to completion of the training programme it had been decided that I should be the replacement 'second dickey'. To go where? With whom? I would be going as second pilot to Squadron Leader J.H.T. Simpson, destination Egypt.

Although I did not want to leave Kitty, I did feel some relief at the news. Most crews would end up on No. 3 or No. 5 Group in East Anglia or Yorkshire, undertaking the far more dangerous operations over Germany or Occupied Europe. I had been one of the many hopeful volunteers for overseas in any case. Had my crew been posted to No. 3 Group then I would have feared the curtain falling on any and every operation. This was something everyone felt but no one discussed. My nightly prayers had included a plea that I might be sent to the Middle East to drop my bombs on the Italians from the greatest possible height. My prayers had been answered in a most unexpected way. I felt, though, as if I had abandoned my crew; Lance, Bill, Gordon, Peter and Geordie. They didn't have a chance to tell me how they had felt, but Lance was a good pilot and became the new skipper, with Bert Battersby as co-pilot.

Before meeting my new skipper I was sent on four days leave. Squadron Leader Simpson and his crew had already had ten days embarkation leave and would return just before I was due back. I had to leave my father's car at Kingsclere. The clutch had gone and I could not await the repair, so it was home by train to an apprehensive Kitty and a very surprised family. Just about all our many relatives had to be visited, and Kitty and I did not get as much time together as we would have liked. I had to make one farewell visit to my aunt and uncle. Aunt was housekeeper to the Dormer Steel family at Chyngton Way on the Eastbourne Road out of Seaford.

When Kitty and I called we were ushered into the drawing room to be introduced to Mrs Dormer, a gracious lady who foretold the future with the aid of playing cards. After introductions she confirmed with me that I was bound for the Middle East, and insisted on reading the cards. I do not remember all that she foretold but she was adamant that I would be going with a red-haired man; we would go via Gibraltar. After seven months I would be shipped home wounded and in some pain. I was rather glad to hear that, as it was from the ace of spades, a much more ominous card, that this last prophesy was deduced. I smiled, but was admonished. 'Young man you will be in much pain.' Then

3

the queen of hearts turned up. 'A light-brown haired young lady will be waiting for you.' Now Kitty was wearing a head scarf, but a curl of sun-bleached hair was showing, a light-brown colour. When we had taken our leave Kitty wanted to know who this light-brown haired girl might be. Her dark-brown tresses were hidden by the scarf. When I left to return to Harwell we were convinced that we would be apart for seven months. The severity of the future wound did set me wondering, the more anxiously as the months passed.

I returned to Harwell on 3rd November and was directed to meet my new skipper and his crew in 'A' Flight office. Entering I spotted a squadron leader with his back to me, and noticed that he was balding fast – so much for the fortune telling. Then he turned around to display a huge red moustache! I was the only one to know his destiny seven months ahead. I was confident of survival for at least that long.

I was introduced to the new crew by Squadron Leader Simpson. They were Pilot Officer Nick Mansell, observer; Sergeant Mick Navin, rear gunner; Sergeant Don Acland, front gunner/wireless operator; and Sergeant Oscar George Ackerman, our number one wireless operator. How I wished that I had been flying out with crew number seven. But these were all likeable fellows who, at that moment, might have preferred their former co-pilot to this unknown quantity.

On 4th November the Squadron Leader was promoted to Wing Commander, and he and I went to Hampstead Norris to inspect our brand new, factory-delivered Wellington Mark Ic, *'ell for Leather*, Z 1041. We air tested it and put it through its paces. At cruising boost and revs it was some 15 mph faster than the Wimpey Ias we had used for training. The turrets were Bolton and Paul with twin Brownings. We were well satisfied.

4

Now, with our first operational flight almost completed, that last eventful week went into the memory. When Gibraltar hove into view we spoke of the turbulence that might catch the unwary round the Rock. The wind was strong and westerly and the neutrality of Spain made an anti-clockwise circuit imperative. Then a long low approach over a grey sea to what seemed little longer than an aircraft carrier. The runway was being extended westwards into the sea, but was far from complete. After a low, slow, steady droning approach Wingco made an immaculate touchdown and we stopped whilst there were still many yards between 'ell and an angry sea. We were close enough to see a salvage operation taking place on an aircraft which had overshot earlier.

On the early morning of 7th November, refreshed and refuelled, we took off for Malta. En route the African coast occasionally came into view as we flew close under cloud cover for protection. However after seven tedious hours the skies cleared and a sharper lookout was needed. The coast was now visible and the Italian island of Pantellaria was not too far away. Then we saw it. It was an Arado flying boat on the starboard beam flying along the coast in the opposite direction. According to the 'Book' it was much slower than us and lightly armed. 'ell for Leather turned to attack. What hair the barber had left on the back of my sweaty neck bristled. This was what we had trained for. However I was soon to wish that we had a reverse gear. There were three more Arados coming along behind. Discretion, overcoming valour, tempted us to use our superior speed to leg it for Malta. We succumbed to the temptation and finally landed on a well bombed airfield after a flight which had again lasted eight hours and fifty-five minutes. Malta was the regular recipient of raids from Mussolini's Savoia Marchettis, and the siege was already on.

That evening the SNCOs of the crew were magnetically

drawn to the Street called Straight, known well by the navies of the Empire as 'The Gut'. It was a narrow walkway between bars and brothels, dance halls and cabarets. At every doorway the exhortation was to enter, for a beer, for a dance, for 'Exhibish' or other female consolation. None of us was inclined to partake of more than a beer in the most well-lit bar. Then we retraced our steps to the 'Poorhouse' where we spent the night trying to sleep on the concrete floor. During that bitterly cold night only a few bombs were dropped. How the next day was spent evades me, but just after midnight on 8th November we got airborne for Fayoun Road in Egypt where, without incident, we landed six hours and fifty-five minutes later. So much for a land that had flowed with milk and honey – it must have soaked into the sand. The odd palm but not a blade of grass! On Armistice Day we left Fayoun Road for Shallufa, our destination on the southern Suez Canal, just north of Suez itself.

RAF SHALLUFA (SOUTHERN CANAL ZONE) No. 37 SQUADRON

Number 37 Squadron, with Wellington Ics, had its base at Shallufa, as had 38 Squadron, with their white Wimps, on maritime operations. It appeared that Wingco's crew had arrived, posted to 37 Squadron. We four sergeants were allocated a ridge tent just north of the parade square, and were utterly amazed to receive but three grotty blankets as our total bedding, the grottiest of the three being a substitute for a bed. No bed, no sheets, no pillow. Our groundsheets went down first on the compacted sand.

The current news on our arrival concerned a recent mutiny by a number of Australian SNCOs just one week before. As a punishment they were to be drilled with rifles in the hot sun, until their sin was purged. However, having formed Flight, at the command 'Slope arms', they had placed their rifles gently on the sand and had stood properly at ease, oblivious to further ranting orders. The Flight was eventually dismissed, the rifles being collected and returned to the armoury. How their disobedience to orders was finally purged, if indeed it was, we never knew. Their original sin? Well, they had been blamed for the inflated contraceptive which floated across the parade ground at sunrise as the Ensign was unfurled at the top of the mast.

From 11th to 29th November we did not fly as a crew. During that time Wingco and Nick Mansell carried out two short raids on the Luftwaffe at El Adem, as supernumeraries with another crew, to learn the ropes. Don, George, Mick and I wrote letters, went to Shafto's the open air cinema, and made sorties on foot to the Suez Canal. On a visit to Suez, George and I were befriended by a Mr Spiteri, a Maltese engineer of the Suez Canal Company, and we twice dined at his house, meeting his wife. On the second occasion we missed the truck back to Shallufa, so spent the night in a little more comfort than usual.

On 29th November we air tested Wellington *D for Donald* of 37 Squadron and on the 30th took off for landing ground 109 up in the blue (desert) prior to an operation. I can't remember where the target was, but record that it was cancelled and we returned to Shallufa via Burg el Arab on the following day. At that time we could not reach targets in Cyrenaica and beyond without first flying to a forward landing ground, where refuelling and bombing-up took place.

On 2nd December we flew to LG 60, thence back to base via LG 09. Why? I don't know. Familiarisation perhaps. On the 3rd we were blooded. We flew to LG 09, refuelled, armed and took off that night to bomb the Luftwaffe and Italian Air Forces at El Adem. It took over five hours, we received our baptism under fire, and I saw our bombs detonate in what might have been the middle of the Libyan desert. I'm sure it wasn't, as I cannot imagine anyone defending the desert so vehemently. I was given most of the flying but Wingco took over for the bombing runs. He was an extremely experienced and skilled pilot with the coolest of heads. I was to be grateful for his coolness but was to curse his courage on many subsequent occasions.

Our second raid was on 6th December. This time we flew to LG 60 for arming, bombed El Adem, returned to LG 09, re-armed and bombed El Adem again. It must have been quite uneventful, though we knew that the Luftwaffe was airborne on our first raid. The idea was to catch them with their pants down on the second sortie. Here we were, the veterans of three raids and only a further 27 to go. We had been baptised so gently into action that apprehension had given way to confidence. With so much that was more memorable to come, the raids on El Adem fade in the memory. That we had been excited is certain. That we were surprised at the streams of lazy tracer directed at us, so that we doubted its efficiency, is also certain. The flashes of the heavy ack-ack and the puffs of smoke left for us to sail through looked unreal and part of a canvas. The relief as the target receded was much more real.

Morale received a setback with the Japanese raid on Pearl Harbor. Two days after the third raid on El Adem we loaded our kit on a truck and proceeded in a staff car, Wingco driving, to Kabret, an aerodrome at the southern end of The Great Bitter Lake. I recall that we passed through the impoverished Kabret village, and were challenged by the sentry at the entrance to the airfield. Having replied to the challenge, Wing Commander Simpson was satisfied when, despite the pronouncement that he was the sentry's new commanding officer, he still had to produce his identity card. That gave us the first inkling of the reason for our transfer to Kabret.

LXX SQUADRON

Kabret seemed to be a more permanent airfield than Shallufa, and the barrack huts were more comfortable. At each end of the long huts there was a pair of single rooms, now furnished to take two beds. These were for the SNCOs but all ranks were supplied with charpoys, wooden bed frames strung with sisal which served as a spring. Mattresses were the three ubiquitous 'biscuits', and it took but a few hours of charpoy 'bashing' to discover that voracious bugs made their homes in the wooden joints, making restful sleep impossible. Some relief was gained by putting 'charps' and biscuits out in the sun, when bugs shrivelled and fell off, but the relief was short-lived. The bugs fell out of the ceilings to occupy the homes of their ancestors. Old soldiers put the legs of their beds in shallow tins of paraffin to create an obstacle to the nomadic bug.

The Sergeants' Mess was a large wooden hut. More bugs occupied the chairs to attack the back of knees. The food was atrocious but we put up with it. Tins of 'Mac Conachies' provided Sunday dinners, the contents consisting of stringy stewed steak, butter beans and potatoes. It was rumoured that an occasional onion had been found. Otherwise it was bread or hard tack, ghee instead of butter, bully beef, sweet potatoes, onions, dates, marmalade, the occasional tangerine, some dried egg, fig jam and the tins of fatty, slimy Irish bacon; or combinations and permutations of any of these.

10

Sometimes a minute real egg would appear, the fruit of a diminutive Egyptian chicken. Bread and fig jam was the usual dessert. I hate figs. The bread was speckled like a currant loaf, the texture rough and grey. The currants were weevils which had found a home in all of the Egyptian granaries, descendants of the plagues I think. Complaints were ignored. Any attempt to pick out the weevils meant starvation. We were informed in Station Routine Orders that the Medical Authorities had come to the conclusion that, since it was not possible to remove the weevils, they were nutritious and could be eaten without ill effect. For a time we tried to live on hard tack biscuits, but concrete would have been kinder on the jaws. We acquired a taste for weevils. Ghee disguised the taste anyway. In fried bread the weevils were crunchy and of a more similar texture. Beer, Pilsener or Stella, was about five piastres a pint bottle (one shilling and a halfpenny). Rumour had it that onions played no small part at the Egyptian breweries. Films were to be seen at Shafto's cinema, with new programmes about three times per week. Peanuts were sold in screws of newspaper. They were unroasted but salted with the residue of an evaporated Bitter Lake.

On 22nd December I was loaned as second dickey to Flight Lieutenant Anstey. His Wellington had a caricature on it of a British Bulldog holding up a Dachshund, suitably labelled with a swastika, by its tail. Now we carried a 'Goorlie chit' written in Arabic to protect us from the Bedouin women, should we force-land, but I wondered what the Hun might do to us if he saw the anti-Nazi caricature. The Bedouin maidens were offered fifty pounds if they returned us to our units with no pieces missing. Had fifty pounds been no guarantee I would willingly have doubled, even trebled the stakes.

With Flt. Lt. Anstey and his crew we flew to LG 60 with overload fuel tanks fitted. The target must have been Benghasi, the Axis port of fame in Libya. It would mean a trip of at least eight hours and the port was well defended. The operation was cancelled, why I don't know, and we returned to Kabret on the same day. At this rate my tour would never be finished.

Wing Commander Simpson took over as Commanding Officer on 23rd December, selected a brand new Wellington Ic, Z1045 *'ell for Leather*, and carried out a consumption test and a W/T test on the same day. He was satisfied since it was a full three miles per hour faster than our previous kite. The news was good. Benghasi had fallen and the Army had driven the Ities halfway to Tripoli. We would soon be moving up into the blue to obviate the need for Advanced Landing Grounds. Prisoner of war compounds were filling. We'd soon be home at this rate.

On 24th December Wingco celebrated his new appointment by detailing himself for a low-level attack on the Hun who was holding up the Army advance at El Agheila, sixty miles south of Benghasi. What a day to risk death! Christmas Eve! We sailed forth from LG 60 at nightfall and droned away for four hours to attack the coast road where we found Ities and Huns moving north, back to Benghasi, in force. We swept into attack, bombing at will. Our gunners kept the Jerries' heads down. Three or four vehicles continued on their way as we came in for our fourth run at 100 feet. Suddenly the gunners stopped firing when they noticed that the four vehicles displayed large red crosses. They were ambulances. Other vehicles turned out to be tanks. Our tracers ricocheted off them into the distance. When the front gunner ran out of ammunition George and I had to man the beam guns, blaze off a few magazines and keep the Hun from retaliating. Finally Wingco was satisfied and we set course for LG 60. The operation had taken over eight hours and it was Christmas Day when we landed, refuelled and made our way back to Kabret and the festivities.

A kip was impossible before Christmas dinner was served in the evening, tired though we were. Each hut had been decorated with a lot of imagination. One was a bar from the Wild West, complete with swing doors. Ours was a grotto with a real river running through. It was fed by hoses from the ablutions. Where the hooch came from I don't know, but the groundcrew, SNCOs and airmen set out to get us sprog aircrew totally incapacitated. They succeeded and I have only a vague recollection of a sergeant fitter airframe, with four years in India and a campaign in Abyssinia behind him, carrying me to my charpoy. I can't remember if I made the dinner, though I believe so. We shared Kabret with 148 Squadron who had Wellingtons Mk. II driven by liquid-cooled Merlin engines. Faster but less reliable, they suffered from coolant leaks and the dust and sand in the air; poor air filters. One member of that squadron was a Sergeant Vertican, a pre-war engine fitter turned pilot. We were to meet him later. Another was Sergeant Iliffe, a member of the Daily Mirror family. His father had insisted he should fly despite his thick-lensed spectacles. We envied him at first, then felt sorry for him. I don't know how it happened but he was to survive a nasty air accident, and was grounded at his own request. I had seen him earlier at Harwell, but I don't know what became of him.

On 27th December we flew to LG 75, an airfield south of Sidi Barrani, well into the desert, to recce the place. It was that 'little bit of heaven fell from out the sky one day', from the old song; just a bit of desert out in the blue. Stony, barren land with a few clumps of camel thorn. Since Air Commodore McLean came with us I was virtually a passenger.

On the morning of 31st December, New Year's Eve, Wingco told us we had been selected for a special operation and would have to fly to LG 60 that day. There we were fitted with an overload fuel tank and half a bomb load. All the way to LG 60 Wingco bemoaned the fact this was not an operation for a married man with children, which tended to worry us a little. Mick was the only other one of us who was married. Where were we going to stick our necks out? At dusk we got airborne and headed north out to sea. Nick the Nav told us our destination; Piraeus in Greece. To do what, I can't remember, but we were to unload some eggs on someone. We passed close to Crete, droning our way through stormy skies. On and on. Nearer to our destination it was snowing and we looked at each other. Couldn't see anything outside anyway. Apparently we began to ice up, and since the target lay in some mountains, totally obscured, we turned round to head for home. Bombs were not jettisoned – we soon found out why. We were to bomb ships in Suda Bay, Crete, on the way back if the main op was aborted.

Now Crete is a pretty hilly place, and lightning was playing ahead. St Elmo's fire had skipped around the turrets and windscreen for some time, and occasional flashes had jumped across the front guns. Wingco said it was quite harmless. Nick, the observer, was a good navigator but I think there was some luck that night in spotting and recognising a landfall on Crete where the clouds were still eight-tenths. After a course alteration we suddenly burst into a clearing at a height of four thousand feet directly over Suda Bay. Nick was in the bomb aimer's position, bomb doors were opened, a target selected and the bombs were gone. Simultaneously Jerry gave us a firework display. We were too low for heavy ack-ack but Breda 88mm guns swept the air all around us. Immediately after the 'bombs gone' there was a crump and a plaintive cry from Mick in the rear turret, 'We're hit!' However he carried on hosing 303s at the ground below. Wingco had to turn and climb out of trouble at full boost, until the bumpy clouds gave us shelter. Then I lurched down to the tail through a heaving fuselage and saw that it was ventilated like a colander. Control

14

cables had not been damaged and ammunition had not been hit. Mick complained of some draught around his legs, but we flew on into clearing skies, landing without further incident at LG 60. On inspection from outside we found at least fifty holes within five feet of the rear turret. The rear wheel was tyreless and the largest piece of shrapnel would have penetrated the bottom of the rear gunner had it not been deflected by the 'D' ring, which bonded the tail together. A new rear wheel and we were back in Kabret on New Year's Day, 1942.

There we were to find that a Canadian had rammed our ablution hut with a commandeered lorry and had then taken off for the Canal Road and Ismailia, picking up some Arab hitchhikers on the way. He overturned the lorry, killing himself and them. His bosom friend, another Canadian rear gunner, said, whilst in his cups, that life was not now worth living. He was to be killed in action in his turret just a few days later. Those were busy days and on 2nd January I was on my way as Flt. Lt. Anstey's co-pilot to bomb the enemy in retreat along the coast road.

On 4th January Wingco took us in his staff car to see Ismailia and I believe we saw *Gone with the Wind* at a local cinema. Returning, we passed a military policeman standing under a palm tree. We were doing 120 kph at the time, slightly exceeding the laid-down 64 kph. Wingco recognised a military speed trap, so round the corner, out of sight he slowed to a crawl. It took ages to reach number two redcap a mile down the road, who was waiting to stop us. Stop us he did – to get a dressing down for his actions. Taking a good three minutes to cover a mile meant the first police-man had to be mistaken, hadn't he? 'Yes Sir,' agreed number two.

At about that time a story in the Forces' newspaper caused some red faces. The *Queen Mary* had brought out a lot of reinforcements to Suez and was preparing for a return trip to New York, unescorted and at better than 30 knots. Old soldiers and airmen, some of whom had not seen Blighty in seven years, were embarking for repatriation. Suddenly an airman went berserk, shrieking, 'I won't go, I don't want to go home,' and he continued hysterically in the same vein. He was soon struggling with two burly military policemen as they forced him up the gangway into custody on board. The *Queen Mary* was approaching Durban before it was discovered that the unwilling passenger should not have been on board anyway! Roll on the Boat!

On 6th January an operation was cancelled whilst we were airborne. On the 8th Eddie Lomas and I took *A for Apple* to BARU (British Airways Repair Unit), Heliopolis, landing over the high-rise flats into the middle of the city. There we had a few days leave staying at a pension and seeing the sights. The pyramids were visited and entered, camels were sat upon, and we got accustomed to the pervasive smells. We travelled on the world's fastest trams from Cairo to Heliopolis and visited the WO's and Sergeants' Club. Here dances with hostesses could be bought by the simple means of plying them with expensive drinks. The girls asked for cider, but moved on as soon as the customer failed to replenish the glass, to a more generous-looking member. The girls had commission on the drinks. They must have been near bursting at midnight when their chaperones turned up. Customers were blotto, but they were quite sober – their drinks were cold tea.

One afternoon I had been looking in a bookshop and had spotted a beautiful edition of Omar Khayyam. It still sits in my bookcase. Having made my purchase I was greeted by the shout, 'Ric!' as I walked into the street. There on the back of a truck was Maurice Tomley, an old boy of Lewes County Secondary School. I climbed aboard to find that he was on his way to an hotel with a few VIPs, having just landed a Catalina on the Nile. Maurice's older brother had been killed in the Battle of Britain – he was a fighter pilot. We had a nose around Cairo that evening, since he was due to take off for Blighty on the following day. Unhappily we got lost. Took the wrong turning off Parliament Square. A young Arab beggar offered a shoe shine. His offer refused, he flicked a loaded brush and scored with a streak of liquid polish across one of Maurice's shoes. By this means a shoe shine was inevitable. However Maurice leapt upon the boy and wiped his shoes clean on the boy's galabiah.

The Arab shouted blue murder, so we retraced our steps at a run, and were extremely lucky to find a horse-drawn gharri which took us back to our respective bug-ridden pensions. I said farewell to him and never saw him again. He was killed within the month. I learned later that his father, Seaford's stonemason, was one of three people killed in a hit and run raid as he was going to work. His mother was then totally alone, having lost husband and both sons in the space of a few months. One could only pray for her, and in those days prayers had to be said before sleeping. There was much to pray for; I had no idea what was happening at home. Two months after arrival not a letter or a message had come. I had written more than forty. The complete lack of contact with home gave me the feeling of having been abandoned. The war was not going well anywhere, especially at sea. My mail was probably on the bottom. However the old soldiers of the squadron were getting the occasional letter some three to four months after posting.

SHOULD I HAVE JOINED?

I had been in the Royal Air Force for fifteen months and my wings were all of five months old. Still a teenager. A great deal had happened since I had sold my treasured Coventry Eagle for three pounds ten shillings. It was September 1940, at the end of the Battle of Britain. With that money I had set out to visit my mother, brother and two sisters who had been evacuated from my home town of Seaford to lodge with some inhospitable distant relatives in Reading. From there I had set out for Leicester where my girlfriend Kitty had been 'evacuated' with her sister and younger brother. I remember little about either visit. In Reading there was no room at the inn and in Leicester the aunt's house was so full that Kitty and I had little if any time together. I soon returned to Seaford where notice awaited that I was required at Uxbridge on 2nd October. I had been turned down by the Fleet Air Arm as too young to be trained as a navy pilot. They had graciously suggested that I might fulfil the role of marine or stoker. I had therefore offered my services as a pilot to the RAF, though to tell the truth, I preferred the naval uniform!

I reported as requested, hair well Brylcreemed, and I was interviewed by three senior officers. *Inter alia* they asked if I had studied trig. for School Certificate. Did I know what a tangent was? 'Some Officers Have, Cash At Home, Till Old Age.' This would surely mean a commission! Did I know

where the Great Bear was? I did? Good. Did I know where
the Pole Star was? I did? Good. You'll do nicely.

On then to a gaggle of medical people, one making me
cough with a surprised look on my face. Another whispered
as loudly as Max Miller, whilst another tested my eyes. Six-
nine, six nine; six-six with both eyes squinting. Fortunately
it was daylight. Next door said, 'I want you to blow in here
for a minute, maintaining the mercury level at or above the
indicator.' Big breath. Blow! The mercury shot almost to
the top, drifting rapidly down to the mark as the seconds
passed. After what seemed to be twenty minutes, eyes a-
poppin', head singing, a voice miles from my pressurised
ears said, 'Stop. Pulse too high. Got a cold?' A miserable
'Yes' from me. 'Come back in a week, come straight to me.
Take this note to the clerk.' After collecting a rail warrant
for 9th October I wound my way home quite miserably. I
practised all week with my cheeks puffed out, under pressure, holding my breath, and on the 9th I returned to the
Doc and his mercury gadget. I blew in the mouthpiece for
all of 10 seconds. 'That's perfect, pulse is low, that will do.'
I never did complete the standard of one minute. Somewhere I swore an oath to King and Country, received a
railway warrant for Babbacombe in Devon, and became
Aircraftman 2nd Class, Number 1268865. I was to swear
many more oaths before very long. I went home for four
days and reported to Babbacombe Aircrew Reception Centre on 13th October. The ominous thirteenth!

THE RECEPTION CENTRE

I remember little about Babbacombe. I'm sure that I would have enjoyed it in peacetime. It was a beautiful spot, soon to provide some unhappy memories. Here I met Bill Bray, who had been an accountant, and, until we had brass and boots to clean, we enjoyed the open air, the many walks and the cliff gardens. Couldn't afford the pubs.

Kitting up is a faded memory. It was rather like a self-service restaurant with no choice. We filed before a long counter whilst NCOs eyed us for size, yelled numbers and initiated the streams of issue to the appropriate scales, which hurtled at us. First a kitbag into which we rammed: pants cellular, airmen for the use of, quantity three; vests ditto; braces, airmen for the use of, quantity one; sticks button; socks woollen, pairs three; and topped it all off with various bits of canvas webbing, haversacks, sheets ground rubber camouflaged, airmen for the use of; and a neat little thing called a housewife, airmen for the use of. I rarely handled her without drawing blood. The Glengarry sidecap which I was given was too large. Luckily I had protruding ears. Worn at an angle it stayed put better, but fore and aft with the lower brass button one inch above the left-hand end of the right eyebrow, it sometimes acted as an aerofoil in the wind, or, settling, left me one-eyed and in the dark. The hairy trousers, made from shoddy, scoured the legs and kept one on the move, It is said that the original shoddy was on its way to the Russians at the time of the revolution in 1917. It was an economic coincidence that this shoddy was still around when the RAF was formed on April Fool's Day, 1918.

At the Reception Centre we were marched here and there, and back, to lectures, to pick up kit, to medical inspections, to meals and when there was nothing to do and nowhere to go we just marched. Our flight was put in the hands of a Welsh corporal, who gave us all the impression that he was parentless, and always had been. One day things were not going well on the march. Several officers had, less than politely, asked our corporal to teach us left from right. Upon the order 'Eyes left' to salute a passing officer, there was a synchronised click. All heads would turn. Some to the left, some to the right, and the rest swinging wildly between the two. Corporal claimed to be a professional boxer and threatened that if we did not hoist our hose he would personally pull each one of us apart, one by one. One or two large recruits grunted in disbelief, since the corporal was but ten stone at the most. Upon this Taffy immediately issued a challenge that he would be in the gym at 1900 hours to accommodate anyone who wished to defy his authority. So far as I know, if he turned up, he waited in vain. Luckily I did not know the location of the gymnasium.

The medical inspection, vaccination and inoculation parade I remember up to a point. Since my earliest experiences with unqualified dentists I had shuddered at the very mention of needles. And here we were marching ever nearer to torture. I can't remember why we stripped; whether it was really necessary or not. My mind was focused on that TAB, ATT jab and vaccination. I had never been done before. During our state of nudity the initials FFI (Free From Infection) were mentioned for the first time. We were inspected, coughing with less surprise, teeth, adenoids, blood pressure, pulse, and then we sat astride forms

21

in a long fore and aft row with our hands on our hips. Ulterior motive? There approaching were three well-armed medical orderlies, syringes at the ready. There was to be no new needle for each then! We were helpless, with no clothes on, shunted up behind each other whilst the avengers went down the row sticking needles in all. I watched one orderly with his cotton wool and rusty nail, and the other two stabbing at every bicep. Stick, push, withdraw; stick, push, withdraw. I should not have joined and passed clean out long before I was stuck. I must have missed a lot of sarcastic remarks but I did not miss the needles. I didn't feel them either. Certain doubts lingered long after I was resuscitated by two nudes in the backyard. Would I ever survive under fire? Suppose blood was to flow, I wondered. The shame lasted the whole two weeks.

The next five days passed with lectures, briefings, drills, marching here and there, or, when there was nowhere to go, just marching. Then it happened. I had a feverish night and was too ill to answer to reveille. Someone sent for the corporal.

'Get up.'

'I can't Corporal.'

'You – get him up – report on sick parade at 0730 hours.'

Somehow I made it, vaccination fever. Back to bed for a day – things must get better, mustn't they? Recovery took more than a day but I was soon on the march again, and whenever we reached the outskirts of Babbacombe we were encouraged to sing:

> I've got sixpence, jolly jolly sixpence,
> I've got sixpence to last me all my life,
> I've got tuppence to lend and tuppence to spend
> and tuppence to send home to my wife.
> No cares have I to grieve me,
> no pretty little girls to deceive me,

I'm as happy as a king believe me,
as I go rolling home.

I've got four pence, jolly, jolly fourpence,
I've got fourpence to last me all my life,
I've got tuppence to lend . . .

And of course the wife was the first to suffer. Well out into the country the songs were other than campfire:

My name is Samuel Hall, Samuel Hall, Samuel Hall.
My name is Samuel Hall, Samuel Hall.
Oh my name is Samuel Hall and I've only got one
      ball,
but it's better than none at all, none at all.

They say I killed a man, killed a man, killed a man,
oh they say I killed a man, killed a man.
Oh, I hit him on the head with a bloody great lump of
      lead,
and now the bastard's dead, damn his eyes.

They say I'm going to swing, going to swing, going to
      swing,
oh they say I'm going to swing, going to swing.
Oh they say I'm going to swing on a bloody great
      lump of string,
just to please the bastard king, damn his eyes.

And now I'm down in hell, down in hell, down in hell;
and now I'm down in hell, down in hell.
Oh now I'm down in hell but what a bloody sell,
'cos the parson's there as well. Damn his eyes.

No. 3 INITIAL TRAINING WING, TORQUAY

Postings came at last. Mine was just a few miles along the road to No. 1 Squadron, No. 3 ITW in Torquay. Bill Bray came with me. How did we get there? Dunno, I expect we marched. My pay was two shillings and sixpence a day, less barrack damages. I don't remember vandalising any barracks. Usually it came to about thirty shillings every two weeks.

A marvellous dentist made a friend of me for life. His surgery was in the St James hotel. He extracted two teeth and filled nine without so much as a single twinge of a nerve. The best filling in my head still remains almost fifty years later. Highly polished. My fear of dentists evaporated.

We lived three in a room at a defurnished Regina Hotel, drilled on the quayside outside the old Spa Ballroom, and again marched all over the place. We learned navigation and signalling, ate at the St James (if we could stomach it), complained only once to the orderly officer, and drank foul tea tasting of bromide. At that time I thought it was to sterilise the water. I think it nearly sterilised mine anyway.

We were fit almost all of the time. Snow lay round about, we trotted up the hill from the Regina, past the signals school to the cliff top beyond. It was very cold. Someone said, 'Bloody freezin', but I didn't swear. We were lined up on four inches of snow facing a grey sea with a cold wind blowing a gale. 'Stand still.' Impossible . . . 'On your backs,

24

down.' He was a bloody sadist. I did swear after all. Flimsily clad bodies were deposited on the snow and legs were waved in the air. Brass monkeys ... fifty of us. After a breathtaking time, 'On your feet. Tallest on the right, shortest on the left, in two ranks, Size' ... 'Ranks right and left turn, ... form flight, ... quick march.' Someone yelled 'Double march,' and we were all soon back in the Regina with the corporal floundering in our wake.

Our flight commander was Flying Officer Pennink, a professional golfer. He was popular with all aircrew cadets, even those not of his class. Suddenly he was replaced by five feet nothing of very rich man. I can't remember his name, but Pilot Officer 'Brass' will do. He was short, probably due to his legs, on the end of which were splayed feet. His head was big, literally and metaphorically. His hat was bigger and his wallet reputed to be bigger still. In the millionaire class. In wearing his Glengarry obliquely across his head he aped Napoleon. Our first rank of three were very tall, dwarfing the flight commander. Cruelly the whole flight copied his march. Corporal Gates, bringing up the rear, could hardly shout, 'Stop mimicking the officer,' could he? We looked like Fred Karno's. Somehow he thought we were taking the mickey, that we disliked him. He was dead right. He got even with us all by detailing the flight for an hour's pack drill under the wing warrant officer who had recently been transferred from Colchester, where airmen were wont to spend 28 or 56 days over the wall. What did it entail? We were soon to find out.

Dressed in No. 1 Home Dress, blue grey airmen for the use of; with greatcoats, full packs, gas capes and gas masks, we drew rifles (but no ammunition) and formed up on the quayside opposite the Regina Hotel. Having formed flight and with arms shouldered we were ordered into a 'by the left, double march'. Surely that 'double march' was a joke? We were so loaded that we could hardly stand. It wasn't long before the weaker, and some of the older ones, keeled over, were removed from the parade ground and were resuscitated in comfort elsewhere. The fit and the stubbornly defiant lurched on, gas capes unfurling and blowing in the wind, gas masks thumping the chest and rifles waving like palm trees in a hurricane. Hup two three four, hup two three four. We survivors glared at the author of this punishment, and challenged the warrant officer to bust his lungs. Rifles fell from tired hands before their owners collapsed. Still the remnants trotted on. Bray was out but Sedgewick was still there. Not much more than half of the flight left. To find that our Flight Sergeant J. Mitcheson had some sympathy and humanity was a revelation. As soon as we got round the warehouse out of view of the warrant officer, Pilot Officer 'Brass', the medical orderlies and the half of Torquay who seemed to be watching, 'Chiefy' implored us to walk a little. We marched about fifty yards, until, just before we emerged into sight he urged us back into the double. The warrant officer did not seem to wonder why the fifty yards out of sight took as long as the hundred yards when we were in full view. At last it was over and all the officers, save one, and all the NCOs without exception, deplored our treatment.

The shirts and underclothes, inside my webbing back pack, were wet from the perspiration which had soaked through vest, shirt, uniform and greatcoat. We were knackered and staggered blindly to our rooms. Had further demands been made on us that day then 'Brass' would not have survived. I doubt if he is alive today. He must have encountered someone of a violent disposition before the war ended even if he never saw active service. Reveille was thirty minutes late the following morning and dustbin lids were banged together very quietly.

Having recalled the name of our Flight Sergeant J. Mitcheson by the simple expedient of reading his signature on the flight photograph, I am embarrassingly reminded of the glorious autumnal day when the flight, all fifty of us, was drilling on the quayside under Corporal C. Gates. All seemed to be going well, if a little apathetically, when there was a bellow from the rear. 'Fall out that man. You I mean.' I just knew he meant me. The rest of the flight were put at ease and I was drilled solo for five minutes. 'Quick march – About turn – Left turn – Ri-i-i-ght turn – E-e-y-e-s left – E-e-y-e-s front – To-o-o the front Saloo-o-ot.' My exhibition got worse and worse. I knew I could not march or drill efficiently or gracefully but it was most unkind of the flight sergeant to yell, in front of all of the flight, and the many amused spectators, 'You look like a ruptured crab!' I felt like one, but that really was quite uncalled for. I gritted my teeth and thought, because I did not swear, 'One day I'll bloody well show you.' I was to get some of my own back shortly but it was a nerve-racking experience.

We had taken and passed examinations, with but four failures. My mark for navigation was on the borderline so that I still wonder who was given credit for my paper. At that time I was much too naive to consider that possibility. We were fitted with goggles, helmets, Sidcot suits, Gosport tubes, flying boots, socks; gloves silk inner, aircrew for the use of; gauntlet left hand leather flying, aircrew for the use of; and gauntlet right hand leather flying, aircrew for the use of. I wondered why the latter were not in pairs and thought that a possible reason may have been the common deformity in aircrew of one hand being larger than the other. Or could it have been that it was more usual to lose one glove than two. Be that as it may, we looked forward to moving on to our flying training. Unfortunately bad weather had held up earlier courses at the Elementary Flying Training Schools. Passing out meant that we were now Leading Aircraftmen and pay was doubled to five shillings a day. Much of this was spent at the Salvation

Army Club on the northern outskirts of Torquay. The increase was considerable to me but did not seem to affect the lifestyle of most of the flight; the 'honourables', ex solicitors, accountants and professional men.

Whilst our further training was delayed we kept up to scratch with signalling, aircraft identification, physical exercises and brass polishing, in between marching. The flight was photographed in November 1940 in No. 1 Home Dress, and in December in full virginal flying kit. Looking at them now I wonder how many, as well as 'The Ruptured Crab', survived the next five years or so.

With the development of the night-fighter it was necessary to find out what the standard of our night vision was. I don't recall any notice but one day we marched to a medical building and, ten at a time, were seated in a blacked-out room, around a ten-sided turret. A clipboard with sectioned paper and a pencil were put into our hands and we were warned to stare intently ahead and draw the items we saw, upon instruction. The lights were switched off. The room was blacker than a locked coal shed on a moonless night. Some put it more rudely.

'First item, draw it.' I saw nothing so drew nothing. 'Second item, draw it.' They were joking. Nothing there. This went on. 'Ninth item, draw it.' Still nothing. 'Tenth item, draw it.' There it was, clear as a bell, a capital C, but backwards. My comrades had been drawing away, I could hear the pencils scratching. I was night blind. This would lead me to fly Spitfires in daylight, I was now certain. It most probably saved my life. Most of those with good night vision ended up on Beaufighters Mk I. These killed a lot of lads. They were prone to ground loop.

Our passing out ball was preceded by an inter-squadron competition. As I remember it included swimming, water polo, cross country running, football and hockey. Our commanding officer, Flt. Lt. F.C. Walker DCM was disappointed with the showing of B Flight, and asked the reason. He was reminded of the unfair hour's pack drill, as some justification. Whatever it was that he promised us for victory must have been alcoholic, and was accompanied by an apology. It was sufficient for us to win the water polo and the first three places in the cross country. We won the competition. The celebration that followed was in the Spa Ballroom. Big Jock saw our diminutive Flight Commander 'Brass' and asked him his fancy. 'A whisky,' was the reply. Jock took orders from all present. The drinks were served, Jock toasted 'Brass' and walked away leaving him to settle the bill! I dare not mention Jock by name, since he was seen later that night in a state of very obvious undress, chasing a young lady round the outside of the Spa. Our pilot officer disappeared on posting during the following week.

There was a cocktail bar not far from the harbour, which was 'out of bounds' to other ranks, save those of privilege. I could not have afforded entry anyway but LAC Crerar made it his evening base, and I suspect that Sedgewick, my room-mate, knew his way inside. My only visit was by general invitation just before our Christmas leave. Try as I might I cannot recall the name of the bar – it began with a D.

In November we were given a 'seventy-two hour pass', starting after duty on Thursday. I made my journey home via Victoria and Brighton, probably on a railway warrant. I remember little of that weekend, but I do remember that I had to be back in the Regina by 23.59 hours on the Sunday. Ever cautious I took an early train out of Paddington, and I remember Newton Abbott, then nothing until I awoke in Plymouth. I had slept through Torquay. Frantic, I was pleased to find a returning train in the small hours. If ever a Ruptured Crab quaked it was then. Quietly I crept up the stairs to my room on the second floor, passing the Orderly room on the way. There I saw our dear flight sergeant fast asleep. In front of him was a pile of passes skewered on a piece of wire. I crept in, lifted a few passes, put mine on the wire and went to bed. He never said anything the next day, but I returned his quizzical look whilst on parade. Almost quits. The flight sergeant still had the edge.

The forty-six survivors of our flight were eagerly awaiting posting to an Elementary Flying School, trying to glean what we could about them. Everything was delayed due to bad weather. Flying courses were behind countrywide, and the Commonwealth Training Scheme was not yet off the ground. Whilst biding time we were marched for miles to make us anxious to buy the instructor a beer at a far away pub. With five shillings a day and beer at fourpence a half pint, life was a lot easier.

Then came Christmas 1940. We were given leave. Once again I remember little about the blacked-out train ride, but I do remember the excitement at seeing Kitty who was back from Leicester, and my family back from Reading, and living at an aunt's house in Sutton Park Road. Kitty stayed with us over some of that holiday and we went everywhere together. We were in love. Some very young acquaintances, seeing LAC propellers, congratulated me on my wings. I did not disillusion them.

As often as we could, Kitty and I sought our own company and shared dreams. It was difficult since the house was always full, and there were innumerable relatives to visit. However in those halcyon and far away days a maid valued her honour beyond price and a gent appreciated that. We agreed that war could separate us finally, and dreaded the day that it might. We loved each other and longed to marry. The war gave extra licence to many but we realised that we were too young. It is difficult to be sure now but I believe that uncertainty was some deterrent. Our destinies, were we both spared, were now linked. Through all that followed faith and belief never wavered.

The morning after I had left for Torquay, a lone raider sprayed Seaford with a machine gun, and dropped a few bombs. Mother told me that a bullet pierced the roof and lodged in the bed in the attic where I had been sleeping.

Upon returning to the Regina we discovered that we were to be moved to the Palace Hotel at Paignton, where we would await our posting to flying training. Our kitbags were taken by truck, whilst we were marched to Paignton 'to save us the walk' so they said. Three members, who knew the geography, jumped a passing bus. Memories of Paignton, where we spent some weeks, are blurred. Reveille at some unearthly hour was heralded by a bugle accompanied by beaten dustbin lids. Frequent celebrations resulted in the discharge of all those fire extinguishers which were recharged, and in hours of forced labour in clearing up the mess. Hand on my heart I didn't do it, but was not excused from the ensuing clean up and bull sessions.

The brother of the huge and rugged film star, Victor MacClaglan, was the Drum Major of No. 5 ITW bugle, fife and drum band. Bandsmen did not do guard duty so I joined as a bugler. Bugling was beyond me as the drum major found out. He was an awesome six feet five inches, a shade off two metres, and I did persuade him that my fife playing would be passable. Truly I could play the band's *pièce de resistance* 'All for a shilling a day', when standing or sitting; but on the march? No chance! There were too many drummers, so I was fired. Guard duties came around with ever increasing regularity. To this day I regret doing Crerar's guard duty, but I had little choice. I was broke, and there was a half crown in it for me.

One day the powers thought that all airmen on holding postings would benefit from a cross country race. Right up my street. Hundreds of us from all the Paignton hotels embarked on a five mile run and I was soon out in front, quite unaware that many were waiting for buses, or drinking tea in the cafés. A mile from home I realised that Crerar, like the proverbial 'puddy tat' was creeping up on me. As he came abreast he seemed much fresher and fifty yards from the finish he took off. I couldn't catch him – second to a wealthy young gent, humiliating! But he was the nicest wealthy young gent I ever knew, and I was to meet this young officer again at Fayoun Road, just after Alamein. He was flying a Beaufighter. To his credit he welcomed our new acquaintance. I hope that he made it. He was good looking, sandy-haired and slightly freckled.

On another day, three of us, encased in our groundsheets, were walking along the promenade in the pouring rain, when we passed a brown job. Such a rude bellow he gave. 'Don't you RAF types salute an officer?' We assured him that if he could convince us that he was an officer we would be only too pleased to oblige. He, too, was incognito under his groundsheet. 'What do you think this is' he shouted, waving a leather-covered stick. Our replies infuriated him, but he was quick to enlighten us that this stick was a baton, officers only for the use of. Our sincere apologies were given to the irate blue blood. Then a smart pace back, a left turn, a quick march and an eyes right in unison was given, to impress this zobit. 'Where's the salute?' yelled brown job. Then it was our turn. 'The RAF does not salute when wearing groundsheets, an eyes right has to suffice.' The vee sign we gave him under the groundsheets was quite invisible.

I don't recall how I came to be notified but it must have been in March 1941 when I received my posting to Sywell in Northamptonshire. No. 6 Elementary Flying School. But Sywell I never will forget.

No. 6 ELEMENTARY FLYING TRAINING SCHOOL, SYWELL

We must have arrived at Northampton railway station en masse. Only a few came from the original flight at the Regina and the Palace, and I remember clearly only two. We were delivered to civilian billets around the town. Mine was with a Mr Ernest Woods, at 94 Ridgeway Avenue, Weston Favell, Northampton. He was older than I by twelve years, with a wife a little older than himself, and a baby daughter Jean, about eighteen months old. He was an accountant, but it couldn't have been a reserved occupation; the reason why he was not in uniform was probably a medical one. For giving me a bed and the use of his bathroom he was paid sixpence a day. He did not have to supply anything else, so I was honoured to receive the occasional breakfast, and to share his living room on those many evenings I did not go out. I was not always in funds enough to sample the Guinness at 'The Trumpet'. The house was an ordinary 'semi' and they were a family anxious for the safety of baby Jean, who slept under a sideboard downstairs. We often sat in the same room listening to the Whitleys staggering off towards the continent at about 110 mph, just an hour or so before dusk. I was to meet Ernest again in 1947 on the Eastbourne seafront. He had gone there for a conference as an accountant to the Northampton Building Society; I saw him again at a new address in Northampton late in the 1960s. He was then a director of the NBS which was soon to become The Anglia. Jean was unmarried, the lady of the house, having lost her mother. Ernest lived but a few years more.

I've rambled way ahead, but I can say that I was not welcomed at first. I was the fourth pilot u/t to be billeted with them, and at least one of my predecessors had been a cad. The two previous airmen had failed the course early, so had left my hosts with a month's peace. I had shattered it.

Each morning it was early to rise to catch an RAF bus from just outside The Trumpet to Sywell. What was Sywell like? Absolutely glorious. We arrived the first morning to be shown into a restaurant dining room, where condescending professional civilian waiters served up the halibut or turbot in large steaks followed, if required, by eggs and bacon. So we were valuable, and appreciated. It made my head swell, unfortunately.

We were given a welcome by our commanding officer, a brand new wing commander who, shortly before, had been the chief flying instructor at Brooklands' Flying School, Sywell. Most of his officers had been civilian flying instructors too, whilst some were World War I veterans. The flight sergeant discip. was a tall young man, little older than I, and had been promoted to that rank directly from Leading Aircraftman, on failing an earlier flying course. With no experience he went by the book – the RAF bible: *Kings Rules and Regulations, and Air Council Instructions.* He carried it everywhere, fully amended.

The wing commander was a gentleman. 'Please don't cause trouble at your billets. Be in at a reasonable hour, comparatively sober, and let me know if the local Air Force Constabulary accost you for any reason when you are in the company of one of the opposite sex.' He ended jocularly with the advice that an airman should always be suitably dressed for the sport he was participating in.

Two cadets were allocated to each instructor. Mine was Pilot Officer James, who introduced himself and gave me a sequence of instructions to paste in the front of the log book which he also handed over. I was extremely disappointed to find that my log book had belonged to cadet A.J. Marsh, and the first two pages had been pasted together and still are. What would they have told me. Did he fail early on? Was he killed? Did they expect me to fail also? I'll never know. The pages remain pasted together.

On 18th March, Pilot Officer James demonstrated the drill to start up the Tiger Moth. I remember the two huge brass-covered switches which cut in the magnetos. 'Switches off?', 'Switches off.' 'Suck in?', 'Suck in.' 'Contact.' And if it didn't start with the first swing or two it was through the whole procedure again. Since '25 mins.' was entered in my logbook in the single-engined aircraft column headed Day Dual, it must have included Item 1, Air Experience. And it was an experience! The cowling rattled, the slipstream whistled through the struts and wires, and the noise was frightening. With great difficulty I heard Jimmy James through the Gosport tubes. He sounded calmer than I felt. 'Feel the movements on the stick . . . Feel it I said. Don't freeze on it.' Except for the holding off in the bank, the controls seemed just as I had anticipated, but the view ahead looked just like a painted landscape. I could look in no other direction yet. Someone was tilting the picture, first to the left and then to the right. Suddenly, coincidental with a lighter feeling in the stomach, the picture was raised just in front of the propeller, which whirred at 1600 rpm. Then, as the stomach forced its way into the lap, the picture disappeared downwards, and only the sky was visible. I comforted myself with the supposition that Jimmy did not want to die, so that, as long as the straps held, I would be alright.

On 19th March it was (1) The effect of the controls,

(2) Taxying, (3) Straight and level flight (nearly), and (4) Climbing, gliding and stalling. Stalling! Help! You knew you were falling but lots of bits seemed to have been left behind. On Monday 24th March it was more of the same, and the log book records a total of one hour and thirty-five minutes. On Tuesday it was 'turns' and on Wednesday 'Taking off into wind' and 'landing' (or trying to land). Thursday was spent in attempting and practising gliding approaches and landings.

On Friday I took off, did a few turns. It was coming. Well it *was* coming, until Jimmy stalled the thing, kicking the rudder hard over. The whole world came up to meet us, revolving the opposite way to the plane. 'Stick forward slightly, opposite rudder, gently back on the stick when the world stops spinning.' It was fun. No way was I going to fail with three hours forty minutes under my belt. I landed the thing, so Jimmy said, as I opened my eyes. On Saturday it was powered approaches and several landings, followed by gliding approaches. Jimmy didn't say he was pleased. Just that he was going on leave for a week and I was to fly with someone else.

On Monday 30th March 1941 I flew with Flt. Lt. Hill. We didn't gel. His nerves were not so good as mine. On Tuesday, Wednesday and Thursday, Flt. Lt. Hill avoided flying with me, but it was more medium turns, take-offs and landings on Friday, for fifty minutes. On Sunday I had a whirl with Pilot Officer Baker. I think I would have been chopped then, but Jimmy came back from leave and we got airborne together on Tuesday 7th April. I then had six hours twenty-five minutes of dual.

What the hell had I been doing? I was worse than when he went away. I had been ready for solo at four hours and twenty minutes. I had four more flights of about half an hour each after that – up, round, down; up, round, down. Take off into wind, climb dead ahead to 1000 feet. Turn to port through ninety degrees. Straight and level a minute or so, turn through ninety degrees to port, straight and level on the downwind leg. With the aerodrome receding under the port wing, turn ninety degrees to port, lose height to six hundred feet, turn port into wind, land straight ahead, unless something was in the way. Then in absolute despair, after several erratic and bumpy arrivals, on 9th April I was handed over to Flight Lieutenant Bremridge our flight commander.

He was a huge man. A veteran of the Great War. 'Now relax, take it easy, pretend that I'm an old gentleman who wants to fly once before he dies.' Hands clammy, muscles in knots, I thought 'Ever a true word spoke in jest.' I believe the take-off was good, the climb OK, downwind alright too, but on the crosswind leg I failed to lose any height, so turned into wind to land at 1000 feet! Not to be daunted it was throttle back, nose down, a screaming dive aimed short of the field, then a levelling off and a reasonable touch down after floating across half of the field. It stuck. Flt. Lt. Bremridge was so heavy it couldn't bounce. I can't remember what he said, but I knew by his tone that the next attempt would be make or break. This time with complete and sweaty concentration all went extremely well and I gently deposited DH 82 No. T 5685, with my old gentleman, just over the hedge, with a three-point landing the like of which I never managed again.

Flight Lieutenant Bremridge must have decided to take the risk. On 10th April after thirty-five minutes of circuits and a spin or two, Jimmy got out of DH 82 R 4773 and said, 'It's all yours, good luck.' Oh help! It took a few seconds to get the mind on track, then, turned into wind, I opened the throttle. What exhilaration, all mixed up with prayers. I believe the solo circuit was copybook. It felt so different with no one in the other cockpit. The Tiger twitched happily about, and it floated somewhat further on

37

landing. It was a wheely, but a perfect one. The most exciting, and almost the most rewarding, ten minutes of my life. I'd done it; in nine hours and forty-five minutes. Poor old Willie Bray hadn't, he was chopped, and another chap from No. 3 ITW had a soloist land on top of him as he was lined up for take-off. The propeller sliced a chunk from his forehead, but he survived. I recall that several Tigers were bent, some beyond repair. Whenever one went up on its nose, one instructor with a little MG sports car drove out to salvage what petrol he could from the crash. With petrol rationed he ran his car on aviation fuel, which would otherwise have been used for cleaning. 'Hard luck old chap, can I have your petrol?'

From then on the month of April was full of hectic flying, with or without Jimmy. Emergency landings, side slipping, instrument flying and low flying, until on 27th April it was aerobatics. Spins, rolls, rolls of the top of loops, full loops, mostly untidy but fun. The airborne gymnastics were easy, it was the landings which found my fingers crossed, but I got away with it. On 29th April I completed my cross country to Cambridge and back. The weather must have been good because I made it. Instrument flying eroded my confidence, though I eventually mastered the turn and bank indicator, and the liquid up 'n' down level. However to watch both of these and a compass at the same time was nailbiting. Always one read incorrectly!

On 3rd May without warning, Wing Commander McKenzie, the commanding officer, gave me my CFI test. I was too naive to realise it was an honour. All went well, save that DH 82 N 5882 was a peach of a Tiger, and my slow roll was the fastest I had ever done, but the nose stayed on a point on the horizon. With only one bounce the landing was one of my better efforts. I had passed, and it was now a matter of clocking up the hours, to a total of sixty.

On one occasion, having warned my ten-year-old sister Pat, who was evacuated to Bedford, I set out to overfly the town, to let her know I was around. Against all rules I looped and rolled and spun over the town, too high for my number to be taken I thought. However, on flying across the town on my way back to Sywell I noticed I was amongst some barrage balloons! What to do, panic! I throttled back, and hung in the air, keeping a keen lookout for cables, and praying. Another lesson, learned, as I landed thankfully at Sywell.

One day I completed a practice dog fight with another pupil quite unofficially, and stuck to his tail like a limpet. In a very tight turn I spotted another Tiger frantically climbing to get near enough to take our numbers. I spun off that turn and whirled down past him. It was three days later when Jimmy said, 'Were you engaged in mock aerial combat last Monday?' I had to nod and was warned never to indulge myself again.

Meanwhile I have glossed over a weekend in April which was, at that time, the most important in my life. During the week preceding Saturday 5th April 1941, I had emptied my post office savings book of all that it contained and, mustering £6 7s 6d in total, I bought an engagement ring at a Northampton jewellers. The size I knew from an earlier check was almost the first knuckle of my little finger. My intention was to go home to Seaford, possibly on the Friday evening, and to ask Kitty if she would marry me. However I was detailed to fly a check with Pilot Officer Baker on Saturday 5th April, and I was not able to get back to my lodgings until about 3 pm on Saturday afternoon. My intention was to clean myself up, collect the ring from my bedroom and catch the train to Euston. However Mr and Mrs Woods were out and the house locked up. After a ten minute wait I decided that I must break in, so up over the outside coal shed and toilet, and into my bedroom I climbed. I spruced myself up, collected the ring, and just as I was descending the stairs the front door opened and in came Mr and Mrs W. They were extremely cross, and wondered how I had entered, but I couldn't stay to explain as the train was due. My prayer was that they didn't inform the RAF police, as my 'weekend' was to be an unofficial one.

There was an air raid in progress when my train arrived, and no trains were leaving Victoria for Lewes or Brighton. The line had been bombed just south of the river. What to do? Someone said that if one could get to Clapham Junction trains would be running from there. How was it to be done? The ack-ack was ack-acking, searchlights were playing, shrapnel was falling and the outside of Victoria Station was deserted. I stood sheltering hopefully under a canopy, feeling, and no doubt looking, miserable. Two thin pencils of light were turning into the station entrance, followed by a red double-decker London omnibus. The driver stopped, looked out and called, 'Where are you going mate?' 'Clapham Junction,' I replied hopefully. 'Hop on then, I'll take you.' He did, driving through the raid as if it was a peaceful Saturday night. I'm sure he wasn't supposed to go to Clapham. There were just the two of us on board but he deposited me safely, said 'Cheerio' and drove off back in to the blitz. An amazing man. He must have preferred to be bombed on the move rather than in a shelter. I never saw him again or knew his name, but I appreciated his courage and my luck.

There was a train for Brighton waiting at the platform and I found one seat in a third-class compartment. There were twelve of us, and no one spoke. All were anxious as the raid still continued. Suddenly there was a thunderous roar, and I hit the floor full length to the utter amazement of my fellow passengers, who were not too slow to dive on top. At least I was well covered should the screaming landmine explode nearby. Nothing happened, all was quiet.

Slowly the other passengers got up and sat down. I picked myself up, realising that what had prompted my action for survival was a train approaching from the tunnel. The doppler effect had caused my red face, and it remained red until Brighton.

Arriving in Brighton I found that the last train had long since left for Lewes and Seaford, and there were no buses. It was 2300 hours. Nothing for it, so with suitcase, gas mask and greatcoat I set off to walk to Bimbo's Garage, Sutton Corner, Seaford, some fourteen miles away according to the signposts. Past Roedean, through Rottingdean, Peacehaven, and ne'er a challenge from any sentry. No vehicles either. Then, at Newhaven at about 0100 hours, I sank on to a seat outside the workhouse. I soon realised that if I sat I would not get up for a long time, so there was nothing for it but to march through Newhaven, cursing that I could not take a short cut along the seashore. That last five miles took well over an hour and it must have been 0330 hours when my mother opened the back door to me. Kitty was staying but wouldn't get up, or shall we say wasn't willing. I don't believe I was too disappointed when I fell into bed, to rise at 1030 hours, absolutely shattered, At 1100 hours I popped the question, received my answer and placed the ring on her finger – 6th April 1941, it was. By 1600 hours I was on my way back to Northampton, tired, extremely happy but wondering what the hell could happen next. I do recall that the anger of the Woods dissipated when I told the full story. I left out the bit about the brave airman diving on to the carriage floor in Clapham.

On another weekend I happened to return a few hours late for the 9 am parade at Sywell. On reporting at the guardroom I found myself on a fizzer, to appear before the commanding officer at 1100 hours. The sprog chiefy discip. marched me in capless, and the CO was charming. However there had to be punishment, and chiefy opened his bible.

Seven days confined to camp would fit the bill he said. So that was the sentence. However, since I did not live on camp the punishment boiled down to reporting to the guardroom before my halibut steak, and before the bus left Sywell at 1700 hours. They could not order me to stay in my billet, since they did not know whether my landlord preferred me in or out of an evening.

Throughout the course we had undergone navigation and airmanship lessons, and continued with our signals practice. We each had about eight hours in the novel link trainer, but Sgt. J Simpson, link trainer instructor, decided I was no LT wizard. 'A fair average, progress reasonable, but rather slow' he said of LAC Barfoot E.A.C. He was probably quite right and didn't think I'd shorten the war. On the course overall the CFI assessed two of us as being 'above average', and I was top in the academic subjects after the examinations. I agreed completely with the CFI, save in one vital respect. He didn't know what a poor sense of judgement I had about the proximity of the ground on landing. I felt for it.

Pilot Officer James asked me what sort of a pilot I wanted to be, and realising my night blindness I quickly said, 'A day fighter pilot.' At the passing-out party Jimmy said, 'I like my pilots to be bomber boys', but he didn't tell me what he had recommended. Then it was farewell to the Woods, who were chuffed at my success, and pleased to follow my progress thereafter. I wrote to them throughout the war. Back to Seaford, and ten days leave, well satisfied. The time passed quickly, most of it in the company of my new fiancée. Still wing-less, but with a whole sixty hours of flying, half of which was solo.

Shortly after I left Sywell an earlier pupil returned in an Airspeed Oxford and shot low across the airfield. He collided with Flt. Lt. Bremridge and a pupil, killing himself and them in an unnecessary display. And the Flight Lieutenant had survived World War I as a fighter pilot!

No. 15 SERVICE FLYING TRAINING SCHOOL, KIDLINGTON

Midway through that leave from 9th May to 20th May, I received a posting notice to No. 15 SFTS at Kidlington in Oxfordshire. I was anxious that the aircraft at that school would be Miles Masters, and was a little apprehensive lest they be those noisy and temperamental Harvards, which seemed to kill off the clumsy. Arrival at Kidlington dispelled the fear. They were twin-engined Airspeed Oxfords. I consoled myself with the fact that twin-engined fighters like the Westland Whirlwind were coming into service, and Oxford experience would be a qualification.

I believe I was billeted in a four-bedded room with LAC Armstrong (who was made course leader), LAC Barber and LAC Frank Beswick, later Lord Beswick (who died in 1988). Frank was older and quieter. he became Minister of Civil Aviation in the post-war Labour government. LAC Barber and I were put under the wing of instructor Flight Sergeant Gilbert.

An introduction to the Airspeed Oxford as depicted on a Player's cigarette card of two years previously was a disappointment. A climb through the small door on the port side and a climb, bent double, up the sloping floor, ended in a greenhouse-like cockpit which contained two bucket seats into which we were to deposit our parachutes and our backsides. There was a strange smell of hydraulic oil. The engines were started by an airman winding a handle as he knelt on the wings. The plane had a retractable undercarriage, but as I remember it the co-pilot had to select undercarriage up or down, and pump. When taxying, taking off or landing the suspension seemed too rigid. Anxiety increased with the rumbles, thumps and bangs. The plane cruised at about 125 mph, and most of it seemed to be plywood.

Soloing after circuits and bumps, and one-engined flying, for three hours and twenty-five minutes, the course seems in retrospect to have been uneventful. Cross country flying, map reading and navigation seemed easy enough as did instrument flying and take-offs 'under the hood'. I did not believe the cadet who said he preferred the turn and bank indicator to the standard flying panel, with its artificial horizon.

Most of our flying was carried out from Weston on the Green, whence we flew daily, or bussed, from Kidlington. Dusk flying merged into night flying. 4th July, Independence Day, was also make or break day. LAC Bibby sat in the co-pilot's seat as I did take-offs under the hood. Later that day Warrant Officer Gilbert (newly promoted) gave me five night circuits and then sent me aloft, alone in the dark, to complete three more safe landings. Well, nothing was broken and my nerves held. I saw little save the paraffin goose-necked flares, but it was a good job they were there. I think the whole instruction staff was suspicious, so that I flew two circuits at night with Fg. Off. Adams, one circuit with Fg. Off. Sparling, and two more with Fg. Off. Adams over the next eight days before they sent me aloft again, solo at night. Survived again. 23rd July 1941, Flt. Lt. Gaynor, CFI test. 23rd July 1941, Fg. Off. Sparling, wings test. 24th July 1941, Fg. Off. Adams, Flight Commander's test. 25th July 1941, a severe reprimand by Squadron Leader Mackie. He insisted that it was I who had almost removed the red warning light from the top of a hangar on landing. To deny it was self-defeating. I could not admit that my height judgement was poor – rather they should think it intentional. I'm *sure* it wasn't me!

On 30th July 1941 we returned to our room to find that Armstrong was commissioned, and we other three were sergeants! There on each bed were two flying brevets and three sets of rank insignia. No passing-out parade. Get 'em sewn on and into action as soon as possible.

I've written little about Kidlington, the course which turned us out looking like Battle of Britain pilots. It was uneventful, but always exciting. Perhaps I was a better flyer than I thought. I didn't think to ask any who had flown me or with me! In any case, the instructors thought 'Average', but couldn't record any special faults! I knew later that what had been a commissioning interview had been quite a disaster – I disagreed with S/Ldr. Mackie in front of the group captain.

I must have spent quite a lot of my off-duty time, and the seven shillings and sixpence a day, in canoeing on the Thames at Oxford. One glorious afternoon the canoe capsized and I was plunged into the water. I had the presence of mind to swim down fully clad to rescue my sinking gas mask, and then pushed the upturned canoe shorewards. At the bank a huge hand was thrust out for me to grip, and I was literally lifted clear of the water and deposited in a dripping condition on terra firma. My rescuer was over six feet, of quite substantial build, with huge hands, and was an Austrian. She was probably a Jewess; she was a refugee, and her name, as one might have guessed, was Brunhilde. I saw her twice more when I canoed without my dried-out gas mask. She was the fastest punter on the Thames, where she was often to be seen punting her guardians. My worry was with my gas mask. Should I own up, and have to buy a new one? Would Hitler use gas? Dried out, was it effective? Thank goodness I never found out, or had to. It stayed with me until I changed canisters with a casualty.

My last flight in the Oxford was on 27th July, and my next was on 15th September 1941 so I must have enjoyed a long leave.

No. 15 OPERATIONAL TRAINING UNIT, HARWELL

I must have had fourteen days of glorious leave, and my chest, decorated with a flying brevet, must have expanded. I can remember that Kitty and I went to Bedford to see my young sister Pat, who had been evacuated there. We swam in the open-air, river-side swimming pool. As a mascot she gave me a small silver-plated Dutch doll which had had a home in a Christmas cracker or a Christmas pudding, and I gave her a 1937 bronze threepenny piece. For the next twenty-six years we were to exchange these tokens whenever we were both in the United Kingdom. I guess they were successful tokens, as we are still around. At the end of my fourteen days leave I kissed Kitty goodbye and left for the station. She hated goodbyes on the platform, and I must have felt somewhat miserable, as well as eager, as the train pulled out. In twenty minutes the train was in Lewes and, whilst stopped at the station, I heard the cry, 'Is Sergeant Barfoot on the train?' I stuck my head out of the window to see who wanted me. The stationmaster himself. 'You can return home, a telegram has been received extending your leave by a further two weeks.' My father had phoned ahead. I don't expect it was early to bed on many of the following fourteen days, but the day came when I passed through Lewes on my way to Didcot and No. 15 Operational Training Unit at Harwell, now the Atomic Research Station. With many others, I was met at Didcot by an RAF coach.

No one spoke, all were wondering why the coach gradually filled with sprog pilots, navigators, and wireless operator air gunners (W/Op. AGs). It must have been four miles to Harwell, and, as it hove into sight, I saw it was a permanent Royal Air Force Station, with married quarters, built in the preceding seven years or so.

The bus pulled up at the guardroom, but before dismounting I saw in the distance what appeared to be a pot-bellied, camouflaged flying pig. Must be a visiting aircraft. A Wellington Mk Ia. I wondered what we were destined to fly. Having booked in at the guardroom, I turned to see the arrival of a second bus. The first chap to get out was a sergeant navigator. I knew because he had proudly sewn his observer brevet on to his greatcoat. We sniggered unkindly as he was told to remove it. Perhaps he put it on his pyjama jacket!

After a meal we were allocated to rooms. I shared one in the Sergeants' Mess. Each had a bed, a bedside locker, a chair, a bedside mat, and a tin wardrobe. My wardrobe had been cleaned out with the exception of a small square envelope, on the front of which was printed 'Durex'. Where had I seen that before? On opening the packet I was glad that there was no one around. Despite my naivety I realised its purpose, and recalled that there was a small automatic vending machine in the Gents at the Buckle Inn, Seaford, which purported to dispense Durex for 6d! Where, today, would you find such ignorance in an eighteen-year-old; or twelve-year-old, for that matter?

The following day we were crewed up. I was part of the following crew. Sgt. Barfoot, pilot; Sgt. Lance Holliday, pilot; Sgt. Bill Reilly, observer; Sgt. G. Howarth, W/Op. AG; Sgt. P. Lord, W/Op. AG; and Sgt. Robinson, air gunner. I don't know the whereabouts of any of them now, but, at a 1981 reunion Sgt. Battersby told me he had seen 'Robbie', who was on hard times 'under the arches'. Lance, no more confident than I, volunteered that I should be the skipper. He was a new graduate of Durham University, so must have been my senior. Be that as it may, they made my crew and I wondered how I could maintain their respect. Since we were destined to fly Wellingtons on night bombing missions I knew I must keep my night blindness to myself.

The OTU kept us busy and on our toes. Some evenings were spent in the 'Horse & Jockey', so far from the main gate that the return journey was exhausting. Here we rubbed shoulders with WAAFs for the first time, and it wasn't long before Lance was chatting to a group-captain's daughter. Her friend was the daughter of a captain, a brown job who had spent years in China, as had she. I believe that her yellow colour was due to TB, and not her affinity with the Far East. On learning that I was engaged she soon found other fellows to chat to.

Our first introduction to the Wellington Ia took place, with the crew, at Hampstead Norris, a satellite airfield on the Berkshire Downs. Flt. Sgt. Gibbs was our pilot instructor, whilst the rest of the crew had their own instructors. The book on air recognition had somewhat mollified my anger and hurt feelings. After all, the 'Wimpey's' cruising speed was 200 mph and top speed was 265 mph, faster than that of my boyhood favourite, the Gladiator. The armament of the Wellington Mk Ia was a twin Browning turret in the rear and one in the nose, but they were not the completely independent rotating turrets of the later marks, by Bolton and Paul.

Emergency beam guns, Vickers gas operated, could be fitted quickly at the beam positions. I believe each magazine contained forty rounds. There were eighteen stations in the bomb bay to winch up bombs or mines, providing the bomb load did not exceed 4500 pounds. Eighteen 250 pounders was a usual bomb load on a shorter raid. There was a lot to learn in the bowels of the plane, but there were priorities, such as fuel systems and hydraulic systems. Whether the Mk Ia had full control of airscrew pitch or whether it had just two positions, coarse and fine, I also cannot remember. Entrance for all the crew was by a ladder through the bomb aimer's compartment. His 'couch' was on the inside of the door. The peaceful way out was by the same door, whilst we were taught that a hurried exit could be made via the cockpit canopy for pilots, via the bomb aimer's position for wireless operator, observer and front gunner, and the rear gunner could, using his discretion, turn his turret to left or right and fall out of the doors at the back. As I remember, though, the latter's parachute was in a rack at the rear of the fuselage, which meant that the gunner would take some time retrieving it. An exit from the canopy could cause a collision with the tailplane, whilst, if the front gunner evacuated his turret he was diced by port or starboard propeller. As a crew we decided to queue up at the bomb-aimer's trap in emergency. The rest of the crew made one stipulation; that I should be last out! Not that I was considered more expendable, but the crew wanted the plane on an even keel for a while.

Our first walk around the Wimpey did not instil confidence. The two huge tyres looked very vulnerable; ballooned and spongy, without any tread. Oil seemed to drip from engines, hydraulic oil from undercarriage. In a wind the fabric covering seemed to flap against odd parts of the geodetic girder-like structure. Patches were stuck on here and there, and doped. All odd colours. The captain's seat was a metal well into which the pilot was to place his parachute-bedecked bottom. A minimum of armoured plating might have protected his head. For the co-pilot there was no protection. A collapsible seat had to be swung into position over the bomb aimer's position. Dual controls were fitted to No. 15 OTU's aircraft. A stretcher was positioned in the body of the aircraft, very near to a chemical closet.

No need to be taken short, or to die standing up. An astradome was positioned midships, in case any observer was ever clued up enough to take sextant shots, but stupid enough to get lost in the first place. The engines were two Bristol Pegasus radials of around 950 hp each.

Somehow between lectures, training on the link trainer and learning the rudiments of bombing theoretical hell out of the Germans, we learned, after a little while, to fly as a crew. Until now, when I think about it, I never realised with what trepidation Bill, Gordon, Geordie and Peter crawled into the Wimp for day and night flights with just Lance and me. If they didn't feel frit, then they must have had a lot of trust in Lance.

During the second half of September, flying from Hampstead Norris, we completed about 24 hours of flying; on two engines and on one; visually and on instruments; mostly by day, but a little by night. Just Lance and me, and Flight Sergeant Gibbs, who was entitled to be, but never was, nervous. The Wellington growled and whined, lumbered off the ground, wallowed into flight, and squatted heavily on landing. The airspeed indicator only exceeded 145 miles per hour in a dive. So much for the aircraft recognition statistics, and *Jane's Fighting Aircraft*. We were told that the Wellington would take an enormous amount of punishment. At that speed it would certainly have to! From the entries in my logbook for September and October it seems that they were recorded by an administrative hand. A lot of detail had been omitted. All because I was wrenched away from my crew and rushed abroad on Bonfire Night 1941. A Pilot Officer Jenner and a Sergeant Jones flew with us on two six-hour flights to see if we could be entrusted with a 'Wimp'.

On 13th and 15th October 1941, having been deemed proficient and worth eighty gallons of petrol an hour, we did a couple of long daylight cross-country flights, during which Lance and I did a lot of instrument flying, with the other as lookout. On 21st October we were bombed-up with three live 250-pound bombs and were briefed to carry out a six hour flight which was to take us to the west coast of Scotland to carry out some gunnery practice in the Irish Sea, and to search for and bomb a target not very many miles south of Bristol. The pilots were to dive bomb the target, one each, after the observer had dropped his from a great height. All went well until we came in over the Severn estuary at 9000 feet, to find this target which was supposed to be on the mud flats. The briefing officer said it was as near an 'O' printed on the relief map as would make no difference. A ten minute search led us to the conclusion that a tiny ring a few yards from the sea was the target, so, from a few miles, with the bomb doors open, Bill Reilly exercised his 'Right, right, steady, left left, steady' until it was 'Bomb gone', and we went down to have a look. He had missed the white circle by a few hundred yards, and that with no enemy ack-ack to contend with. As we got lower we could see sheep dashing about. The white ring was of stone and was a sheepfold! Luckily only the sheep were there to complain. However, whilst investigating we passed over a yellow buoy which was floating in the sea. We realised our mistake. No one had said anything about the tide coming in. Lance and I bombed the buoy, failing to sink it, and repaired for Harwell post haste.

I enjoyed a few weekends at home financed by a lucky streak at a game called brag, with black deuces wild. Our pay as sergeant pilots was thirteen shillings a day, or four pounds eight shillings and ninepence a week after deductions. After one such weekend I returned with 'Agatha', my father's fourteen horsepower Morris Oxford, and the crew had an earthly chariot. One evening we journeyed to Reading and with considerable Dutch courage, invaded a Civil Service Ball. Apart from us everyone was in evening dress, and very formal. We were tolerated because we did behave, and were invited to dance. I'm no Fred Astaire but I found myself spinning at speed with a very civil servant who, catching sight of herself in the wall mirrors, and appearing 'leggy' stopped the spin by the simple expedient of tripping me up. My apology went unaccepted.

On another occasion, after a local hop in Didcot, the crew piled into 'Agatha' and we set off for Harwell. The car almost stalled at every incline and I suspected that the mechanics were duff. We struggled on for four miles, but finally came to a halt on the incline outside the Married Quarters. There was a rattle on the roof and numerous scuttling feet. The car picked up speed and I have no idea how many passengers we had carried externally, on roof and rear carrier.

Petrol was rationed. My ration was seven gallons per month, but that was no worry. The local garage proprietor in Harwell village managed to cover the sale of a few buckshee gallons with coupons from the local farmers. Ten extra gallons could be obtained for thirty-five shillings, at double the legal price. The whole crew had a whip round for the extra. The garage owner had a good thing going. (Well he did until early December when he sold some black market petrol to the Customs and Excise, at an inflated price. He may yet be inside.)

On 26th October 1941 all crews were briefed to undertake an exercise, a night cross-country flight, flying from beacon to beacon, to the north of Scotland, returning down the Irish Sea. There we were to drop a flame float for the rear gunner to take a drift. The navigator would calculate the wind velocity and the gunners would proceed to shoot out the flame. Thereafter we were to return to a bombing range, drop a few practice bombs singly and in sticks, before returning to Hampstead Norris. The dropping of a stick of bombs was controlled by a clockwork Mickey Mouse, something like a clockwork timer. A small arm would traverse the face of eighteen contacts, at the press of a button, so releasing the bombs from the bomb bay in a regular sequence. The speed of the arm could be altered to adjust the spacing between each bomb. All that day the weather had looked threatening and, since the flight was to involve the use of oxygen at a height of over 10,000 feet at some stage, cloud flying in freezing conditions might be involved. The wireless operator, under the watchful eye of an experienced 'sparks' would be needed to take bearings from radio beacons. The navigator would be involved with a lot of dead reckoning to calculate our position.

Bill Reilly was a good navigator so Lance and I had only to drive to his instructions. Robbie and Peter checked their guns with anticipation and some foreboding, doubtless praying for a cancellation. It didn't come. At dusk we piled into buses and were driven past the 'Horse and Jockey' through East Ilsley, to Hampstead Norris. Quietly we climbed into Wimp 9809, and went about our respective checking duties.

Came the time to start up. I could only liken the noise of the 'peggies' to a thousand of the old-fashioned cast-iron mangles operated by as many fit Chinese in a laundry. Certainly the noise was not a healthy one, the engines sounded very worn. For a short while flames licked out of the masked exhausts. With engines warmed up we watched as Wellington after Wellington lumbered and fidgeted its way to the leeward end of the runway, turned, curtsied as the brakes were applied and rumbled and roared until the brakes were released. The thousand mangles were replaced by five thousand as the engines strained to enable the plane to reach eighty miles an hour before the end of the runway was reached. Navigation lights twinkling, each circled the airfield before proceeding on track. Then it was Crew No. 7's turn. I was so grateful that others had gone before me and had signposted the way between what seemed to be a haphazard scattering of goose-necked flares. Had we been first then Lance would have had to guide me in the taxying. Outside the sky looked stormy and it had started to rain. Inside there were more apprehensive hearts than confident steady ones as 9809 lurched, lumbered, curtsied and dawdled under my inexpert handling of the throttles and brakes. At last we were in a position across wind at the end of the runway, waiting for the green Aldis to signal the off. The intercom was quiet. Instrument lights were turned down to a minimum. Gauges were checked. Airscrews were put into fully fine, and mixture into 'Rich'. Behind me Bill Reilly turned down his chart table lamp and strapped himself in. Peter lay on the stretcher aft, as the front turret was wisely unmanned for take off. Whether Robbie was in the rear turret or not I had no way of telling. Perhaps since the weather looked so threatening we'd get a 'red' to call it off. 'There's the green,' said Lance, and he sounded intentionally calm. 9809 turned into wind, throttles were opened to the stops against a tightened throttle nut. The brakes were suddenly released and the fabric-covered motorised Meccano set stirred and lurched forward.

At forty-five miles an hour the tail responded to forward pressure on the control column, and the wheel that Robbie should have been sitting over became unstuck. Still the huge balloon tyres kept us lurching with the contours until flying speed of about seventy was reached. Another couple of hundred yards and I synchronised a sigh of relief with triumph as we missed the boundary and sailed off on our adventure. A sweep round the field, climbing, then on to course. Bill had preset the compass. For a very short while our home beacon could be seen and, through a gap in the clouds, we could soon read the next one ahead. Then it was into heavy rain and on up into enveloping, bouncing blackness of a particularly rough kind of cumulus. Outside the cockpit the exhausts glowed despite shrouded flame shields.

The IFF ('Identify Friend or Foe') was switched on to avoid any mistakes, and the navigation lights were switched off. Bill switched up his chart table lamp, and Gordon Howarth twiddled his knobs and listened in. 9809 brushed aside the obstacles in the sky and moaned on. The engines had to be synchronised frequently to obliterate the beat, and Lance and I took turns at the controls, the other keeping a watchful eye on the instruments and handling the fuel controls in the fuselage. Spare engine oil was carried in a tank on the starboard side of the fuselage, and frequent pumps had to be made to the handle supplying lubrication to our power plants. Natural relief was attended to at the Elsan which was bucking about somewhere amidships, and, since there were two pilots, the funnel-ended tube clipped under the skipper's seat went unused, so that no acid rain fell on our account that night.

The driving needed considerable attention and, as we climbed into blackness, the exercise was one of dead-reckoning navigation. We trusted Bill but clawed high enough in the sky to avoid two Ben Nevises, though we were supposed to be nowhere near it. Gordon and Peter took turns at the wireless set and managed to supply Bill with bearings from the National at Daventry, and other beacons, despite the static interference. Stomachs felt alternately heavy and light, or light and then lighter as we droned on. Bill, who often stood at the chart table, sometimes left the floor. The talking was probably inversely proportional to the praying. At the dead reckoning turning point we headed south, still buffeted by turbulence, and, when Bill was sure, when he had convinced the other six on board, we let down over the Irish Sea, somehow missing the Isle of Man. At eight hundred feet we saw it – the sea, foaming white in no light. Well, I didn't see the sea actually but did see some of the fluorescent foam. Then we dropped our flame float, whether down the flare tube or from the bomb bay I don't remember. Robbie took drifts on it with his rear guns, reading the drift from a scale on the inside of his turret. By utilising our airspeed, course and drift, Bill was to work out the wind speed and direction. Whatever he made it, he didn't believe. Then the gunners tried to extinguish the float with several bursts of machine-gun fire. They didn't, but were close enough to frighten the thing. Then on course, we went into the climb to clear Snowdon by 3000 feet, and once more back into the murk. Robbie took a nostalgic drift on the flame float as it disappeared from view. Almost on schedule, to Bill's instructions and to our surprise, we let down, and in a clearing between clouds saw and recognised a beacon. We changed course for the bombing range. Far from the bombing range being a circle of goose-necks, there was barely a semicircle left. Obviously earlier crews had scored some direct hits, so we made run after run, dropping single practice bombs, then two sticks, from a fairly low altitude. The crew reported on the flashes from the ground, and we were rewarded with hits inside the semicircle, although the goose-necks burned on. 'Bombs gone', and it was back to Hampstead Norris. Our worries were not quite over, I had to get down in a blackness cheered only by two rows of paraffin flares below.

A QFE (a request, transmitted in Morse code, for the barometric pressure) had been sought by wireless telegraphy (W/T)), and had been set on the altimeter. A good job too, because the pressure had dropped considerably and we might have landed at 500 feet above ground. The circuit was accomplished. Hands were sweating and eyes peered intently at the approaching flarepath. Before I could apply a little more power, 9809 swept over the end of the airfield, between two enormous elms and plonked itself on the runway. Bill Reilly, who had been standing in the astradome against all rules, had obviously seen the trees more clearly than I. As we disembarked he was overheard to say, 'What idiots planted trees at the approach to the runway?' We were taken to the debriefing hut where the bleary-eyed officer remarked on the foul weather. We agreed that it had been very rough, 'even ducks were grounded'. 'And so would you have been if you had heard our recall after half an hour.' With mission accomplished, and despite the fact that Peter and Gordon had missed the recall, we felt extra pleased and perhaps cocky to have conquered the weather. If we had been off to Cologne, the Hun would not have expected us on such a night. So no one else had bombed the target after all, and we awaited the answer to the intelligence officer's landline call to the bombing range, to verify our claim of several direct hits. The answer to his query was not at all complimentary. It seemed that the airmen were extinguishing and picking up the flares at the time of our mini-raid. They had only just returned from a frantic dispersal in the 15 cwt truck, to inform their commanding officer that training for war was as dangerous as the real thing.

We had a good look at those trees which we had missed, on the following day. They were all of one hundred years old and one hundred feet high, so had probably been planted without consideration of the danger to pilots under training.

My school chum's family, Eddie, Joyce, Vi, and their mum and dad had moved to the village of Kingsclere, not far from Newbury, a short haul from Hampstead Norris in a Wimpey. I'm sure only Lance was with me when we shot by their house in the Dell at bedroom-window level. In fact I saw Mum waving at the window, and Joyce waving from the front garden as I narrowly avoided a hillock and swept over the Observer Corps Post in the meadow. Had it not been for the fact that Eddie's father supplied them with water from his well, and beer at the 'George and Horn', I'm sure I would have been reported. I promised I wouldn't do it again when I met them for darts a few days later.

road. On 15th January 1941 we air-tested *'ell for Leather*, packed our kit, said our farewells and departed as a squadron to LG 75, south of Sidi Barrani. A fuel dump, some vehicles, bowsers for petrol and water and a big pile of tents and stores awaited us. The desert war was going well and we would be moving up to take over El Adem soon, so our tents were not dug in. EPIPs (English Pattern Indian Patent – a small marquee about 15 feet square) were put up for offices and mess tents. We were not trained in logistics. Had we so been then we would have worried more about the water supply. There was none. One highly brackish and chlorinated bowser of water, 400 gallons, appeared miraculously each day to supply the needs of the whole squadron. Each man was rationed to a quart water bottle per day and two mugs of chai. That was the biggest hardship. It allowed one wash or lick a day and we soon all followed the same routine. Drink half of your tea at breakfast, brush teeth in two mouthfuls, shave in the rest (it was better without sugar). Wash in a cup of water, rinse in a half cup. Save both lots of used dirty water in a four-gallon petrol can, a shiny tin, cuboid-shaped. In the evening the whole mug of tea was drunk to assuage a day-long thirst. A modicum of water was taken from the water bottle to clean teeth. In that way almost a full water bottle was available to accompany each aircrew on operations. There were special racks in the Wellington to hold six water bottles. Each rack was labelled. Gradually the four-gallon tin would fill, and every few days one would manage a bath or rub down, as much water as possible being saved. At the end of a week we washed our clothes in the many-times-used soapy dirty water. Before refilling the water bottle each morning we drank whatever brackish water was left. Our whole life seemed to revolve around the supply and utilisation of one quart of water and two mugs of tea. The camp was dry and dusty, not very warm at that time of the year, but prone to frequent sandstorms. Comfort was at a premium when a sweaty body was pestered by flying sand. Prickly heat and ulcers were commonplace. Beds were our groundsheets on the stony desert, and 'charpoy bashing' was again a number one pastime. Egyptian PT (Egyptian Physical Training) they called it!

Four days after our arrival at Landing Ground 75, on 22nd January 1942, we set out to attack the Jedabaya Road, south of El Agheila. We were carrying an overload tank, and the idea was to use the overload tank first. A quarter of an hour out, whilst still climbing, Wingco sent me back to switch on the overload and turn off the main tanks, something I had done many times before. What happened I don't know, but a few seconds after I turned to go back to the co-pilot's seat both engines cut. I dashed back to switch on main tanks as Wingco opened the bomb doors to jettison the bombs. Both engines picked up immediately, but with 'bombs gone' we returned to base. Next morning it was pointed out to us that our bombs were still in the bomb bay, and we broke into a sweat. Eighteen-inch rods had been fitted to the nose fuses to convert the bombs to anti-personnel. The bombs should have exploded above ground. However, even on safety they would explode with rods fitted, and many a crew had been lost in a prang with rodded bombs aboard. Whether I had made a mistake with the fuel cocks or not, I was not interrogated, as Wingco had erred in landing with full fuel and bomb load.

We were given a weekend pass for Alexandria, and travelled all the way along the coast road by truck. Our club accommodation was good and clean. We shopped and went to the cinema, buying a few meals and avoiding Number 5, Sister Street, the infamous address mentioned by many a navy man. Our return was a few hours late but a cast-iron excuse did not prevent us from being officially reprimanded by our own skipper. Promotion was thereby put back for three months. But that wasn't the worst thing. Some klefty-wallah had stolen at least two gallons of my dirty and soapy water which I had been saving for a bath and my dhobi.

Three days later we again set out for the Jedabaya Road, and there were no mistakes this time. We bombed the German lorry parks, tanks and convoys with impunity from about 300 feet, destroying motor transport and armoured cars. Then it was down to fifty feet with all guns blazing. The enemy kept his head down. I think that the tide was turning on the ground in the enemy's favour because two days later we found that Jerry, on the Jedabaya Road, was returning towards Benghasi, which had fallen around Christmas Day. Once again we bombed at will, unable to miss the parks of trucks. This time we spent an hour over the target at low altitude using bombs and guns selectively. Again on 30th January 1942 we set off for the same target, since the German advance had started. The bombs were dropped on the road in one stick, gunners blazing away simultaneously. Several strafing runs were made, but it was when the front guns jammed that Jerry opened fire. A lazy tracer floated into the bomb aimer's position with a shower of sparks and a bang two feet in front of me. A small fire started forward on the perspex under the front turret. I grabbed at my water bottle and was surprised to find that its neck had been blown off. To extinguish this small fire I did not even have to remove the cork! We were already climbing away from trouble, but could see 88mm tracer shells floating by under and over the wings. They missed and we made base in record time to find that we had also been hit in the rear. One of the front gun barrels had an armour-piercing bullet jammed in it. From that day very few armour-piercing bullets were allowed to be fitted in the belt, since they wore out the barrels. *'Ell for Leather* was due for a forty-hour double star inspection, as well as fuselage repairs, so I flew it back to Kabret on 31st January, where I stayed for a few days until it was ready for air test on 4th February. It was great to get a bath, to sit in the Mess, and to feel the bugs again but, best of all, I found many letters in the letter rack for me, the first I had had since leaving England on 5th November. They had taken three months. A long search through the racks and I had hundreds of letters for the boys up at LG 75.

The air test was to be a formality; just a flip around the Sinai desert, so, lined up on the runway I opened the throttles and *'ell* gained speed towards the Suez Canal. What on earth was happening? Faster and faster we went along the runway, but the air-speed indicator showed no more than 50 miles per hour whilst the altimeter was racing round clockwise. Halfway down the runway and it registered over 50,000 feet. The ASI had been connected to the static side of the Pitot head, and the live side to the altimeter! Too late to stop, so it was into the air to fly by look, feel and the seat of my pants. The final landing was from a very low approach at a very fast speed; but we stopped before reaching the canal. The error was quickly rectified, the fitters admonished, but our take-off for the blue was delayed. On the 6th February we received orders to make for LG 104, just three miles west of El Daba along the coast road. Jerry had broken through. Our move to El Adem was off, and we had retreated about eighty miles to LG 104. On arrival, after a flight of two hours, we were given an eight-foot-square ridge tent, had a piece of rocky desert allocated to us, and were told to dig ourselves in. Pickaxes and spades made little impression, maybe four inches on the first day, and less on the second. We erected our tent over the hole and prayed that Jerry would not pay us a visit. He did. On the second night he bombed and strafed us. I envied the Flight Sergeant armourer, who had blasted a hole for his tent with explosives. We could stand it no longer. Don, George, Mick and I made a run for the beach, there being a good moon. We returned when the bombing and strafing finished and walked back at dawn to continue our digging for another few days, until we reached a depth of about two feet six inches. Then we dug a slit trench, covering it with some old bowser doors. The ground was very rough and hard, but we felt safer dug in. After the last strafing and bombing many tents were in ribbons but no one was hurt. We had been warned by the ground gunners manning the Lewis guns that they would shoot us if we ran for the beach in an air raid again! The 'ground-gunners' had been selected and trained by a Flight Lieutenant Jones, who was at least sixty years old if a day, white-haired and a veteran of the Great War. Had we run again whilst strafing was going on, the gunners would not have seen us. They kept their heads down too low behind their sandbags.

Came the day that I had to act as escort to the ration wagon which went down to the NAAFI warehouse at El Daba, and there I spotted a heavy discarded table which I purloined and took back to camp. It was an old butcher's table. The top was six inches thick and well worn by axe and knife, but it did for my bed. Unfortunately the top was just at ground level in our dugout, and I had to roll under it in the event of an enemy raid. I never did shorten the legs!

The aerodrome was on a cleared flat piece of land between the road and the railway, whilst the camp was between the road and the sea, on a rise. South of the railway was a South African squadron of Maryland bombers. The Sergeants' Mess was a huge blasted hole covered by three EPIP tent tops but, before it was put to use our mascot, a contented Egyptian hen, was put into it with the cockerel which was the South African mascot. All gathered to witness the outcome. The cockerel crowed strutted and approached time and time again until Matilda struck out and chased the South African intruder. He easily flew out of the eight foot hole, and fled, chased by his keepers. Matilda preened and tried to crow.

From LG 104 we were able to bomb as far afield as Benghasi, but an overload tank was still necessary, and the bomb load for such a journey was four 500-pound bombs and one 250-pounder. Benghasi was raided five times and Martuba, south of Derna, once by 5th March 1942. On 14th March the whole squadron was bombed-up, and at briefing we learned that our target was the Italian aerodrome of Calato Lindis, just landward of Rhodes harbour.

The journey was uneventful, but as we approached Rhodes at about 10,000 feet we could see that a terrific anti-aircraft barrage was being put up over the harbour. Heavy ack-ack was bursting at all heights and Breda 88 mm guns were hosing up tracer shells. We thanked our lucky stars that another squadron had the harbour as a target, and, skirting the town by a few miles, we made several bombing runs over a poorly defended Italian airfield. The defensive barrage over the town and the harbour was terrific, and we could now see frequent explosions on the waterfront and in the town. We wondered who were the unlucky recipients of all the flak. On our final bombing run I was startled to see just two rows of tracers skimming over our starboard wing, not fifteen feet from me. Our rear guns opened up and, on the end of the tracers, a Fiat Cr 42 biplane sailed by out to starboard with not many more knots on the clock than we had. The front gunner bade him farewell with a long burst. We kept our eyes peeled against his return, but didn't see him again. Bombs gone, we made our detour, watching flak and bomb bursts in the town, grateful for our escape, and landed at LG 104 after five and half hours. At debriefing we could not find out who the unlucky squadron was, nor how many aircraft had been lost. The intelligence officers hadn't a clue, and we would never have found out but for the fact that it was printed in the Forces' newspaper, *The*

Union Jack, three days later. The 'squadron' detailed to bomb Rhodes harbour was a flotilla of three destroyers. Whilst our squadron was circling the town and bombing the airfield, shells from the destroyers were landing on harbour targets. The defenders, hearing the Wellingtons and conscious of the bursting 'bombs', just hosed the sky with all the guns they had. There was nothing up there! The news was not broken until the destroyers had returned safely to Alexandria. Seventy Squadron had acted as a diversion. I later met some of the navy men on that operation. They were pleased to know we had seen their shells bursting, since they were adamant that they were firing blind. Blind drunk.

Letters from Kitty and from my parents were arriving in batches, letters written without any knowledge of my health, since my letters had not reached them at the time of writing. I was writing three times a week. All letters, save for one a month, were censored on the squadron by the orderly officer so contents were inhibited. The monthly letter was put in a special envelope which was liable to censorship at the Army Post Offices. Airgraphs were then invented. We wrote on a special form about nine inches by six inches. These forms were photographed, and transferred as 35mm films to the UK. There they were printed up to a size about four inches by three inches, and delivered to the addressee. Magnifying glasses were often needed since the writing on the photograph was about one third the size of the original, and we all wrote small, to get as long a message as possible.

Food was still a permutation of bully, weevily bread, hard-tack, fig jam, dates, sweet potatoes and ghee, with occasional marmalade. No one ate the dates. Day after day the sticky mess occupied the centre of each trestle table, acting as a fly trap. We didn't mind. Whilst flies ate our dates they left us alone.

On 28th March 1942, with Jerry blockading Tobruk, and

subjected to bombing raids from the Junkers 88s, we bombed one of their airfields at Martuba. There was little opposition and damage was slight. Wingco called a conference on 29th March where it was decided that on our next airfield raid we would each have a height and, at a certain time when all were circling the target, we would each start our run in a predetermined direction. This was put into effect on 30th March with a raid on one of the landing grounds at Derna, where a new Luftwaffe squadron had arrived. Each Wimpey was bombed up with eighteen 250-pound bombs, all fitted with anti-personnel rods. Over the target *'ell for Leather* made the first run at a selected height in a north-westerly direction. The bombs were connected to the 'Mickey Mouse', ensuring that all eighteen bombs fell in a stick over a mile. 'Bombs gone', and we watched the ground as the aircraft steadily lightened. Whoompf, whoompf, whoompf – eighteen times. A great row of holes appeared across the enemy airfield. I had previously been on the other end of a smaller stick of enemy bombs as they exploded nearer and nearer, so I knew how Jerry was feeling. Bomb number sixteen hit an aircraft, seventeen set two more alight and number eighteen hit the fuel store. Four glorious fires to aim at and the other eleven Wimps came in turn to bomb, each with a covering stick of eighteen bombs. We circled, watching, as the airfield was turned into a moonscape littered with fires. Two hundred and sixteen bombs wiped out that airfield, and a PRU (photo reconnaissance unit) Spitfire photograph showed an almost perfect Union Jack covering the landing zone and terminating near the aircraft dispersals. The Luftwaffe unit was almost totally destroyed.

Between operations Oscar George Ackerman, our wireless operator, and I made our way each day down to the beach, through camel thorn and sweet-smelling scrub. The sea was always calm, always blue and there was no one about, not even an egg wallah, so our nudist beach stretched from Alexandria to Morocco. We only used a small bit of it. We would spend hours on the soft, white, undisturbed sand, with occasional dips in the briny. I learned that George had been a repesentative of the American Tobacco Company in China before the war. He spent his schooldays at Brighton College before several years in Manchuria and China. Life had been very good to him. He was paid well and had quite a knowledge of Japan and the geisha. With the outbreak of war he had packed his belongings, including a good collection of ivory. He had left the trunks in a warehouse belonging to the American Tobacco Company. He had set out for England early in 1940 and, during his training in Blackpool, he had billeted with a Mrs Simpson. Here he had met and fallen in love with Jean, the eighteen-year-old only daughter of the house, and had become engaged. He wrote as often as I did, and sent Jean a gold charm for her bracelet as often as we could visit the Delta.

My story was not so worldly and he soon elicited the fact that I was without experience. I don't think it affected our understanding. I sensed that he might have wished that he had met Jean earlier, when he had been younger and less worldly. He was well spoken, and of good physique, an inch or two shorter than I. We lay face down on our towels spread on the warm, soft sand and dreamed of the day that our tour of thirty operations would end. And we dreamed of afterwards. Such dreams were fully arousing with a deep longing for home. Until this time I had fully expected that I might not return, but now I was determined to live, if I possibly could. There were two months to go before I was due to be wounded, and invalided home, as the cards foretold.

On the night of 6/7th of April 'ell was bound for Benghasi harbour yet again, an operation known to us all as 'The

Mail Run', and remembered in a song to the tune of 'Clementine':

Down the Flights each bloody morning
sitting waiting for a clue
same old notice on the Flight Board,
same old target, guess where to.

(Chorus)
Seventy Squadron, Seventy Squadron,
though we say it with a sigh,
we must do this bloody Mail Run every night, until we
    die.

Take off for the Western Desert.
Fuka, 60 or 09,
same old Wimpey, same old target,
same old aircrew, same old time.

(Chorus)

Navigator, have you lost us?
Come up here and take a shuft,
Someone's shot our starboard wing off,
We're alright, then, that's Tobruk.

Forty Wimpeys on the target,
Two were ditched down in the drink,
Then three others pranged on landin',
Bloody hell, it makes you think.

Fighter coming into starboard,
Bloody Hell we'll have to shift,
Find the bloody gunner sighting,
On the fighter for a drift.

Stooging round the Western Desert,
With the gravy running low,

Wish to hell I could see Fuka,
In the shit storm down below.

And old Tennant from his photos,
Said we seldom reached BG,
Sees no bombholes in the roof tops,
Only craters in the sea.

Try to get your thirty ops in,
Without your Wimpey being hit,
If you do you'll go to Blighty,
If you don't you're in the. . . . !

Oh to be in Piccadilly,
Selling matches by the score,
It might be a little chilly,
There'd be no Mail Run any more.

There were earlier and later versions but this was the
Kabret-based special. Benghasi was a long trip, well known
to all the Wimpey squadrons. I think it was 38 Squadron
which was detailed to lay mines in the harbour, and just
outside, for night after night. They ran out of mines, and it
is rumoured that tail fin containers full of sand were
dropped in lieu to keep Jerry's mine sweepers busy. Then,
it is said, 4000-pound bombs fitted with seventy-two hour
delay fuses were dropped in the harbour, in the hope that a
ship might be near enough when the big bang came three
days later.

We set off to Benghasi on 6th April with the usual
overload and with four 500-pounders and a 250. As I
remember it, the night was without a moon but cloudless,
and after three hours we started to climb just as high as 'ell
would go. At 13,000 feet we approached Benghasi harbour
from the sea. Only the radar-controlled heavy ack-ack could
reach us, although the searchlights caught and held us on

the bombing run. Wingco was determined to take a good night photograph, so it was my job to set and release a photo-flash bomb down the flare chute, when ordered. The camera shutter was opened as soon as we had escaped the searchlights, bomb doors were opened and the navigator concentrated on his bombing run. I could see nothing but bursting shells, feeling the occasional crump. 'Bombs gone, one two three four five six, release the flash.' With pleasure! It shot down the tube, the lanyard pulling the clip and setting the fuse. A blinding flash at about 4000 feet, and the camera shutter was closed. The ack-ack stopped, generally a sign that a JU 88 was in the vicinity, so it was nose down and a swift departure at a rate of knots. I flew her back but started to feel a poke. Nick pointed to the altimeter. I had dozed off, and allowed the kite to come down to 1500 feet! I'm sure Nick didn't tell Wingco, who was fast asleep in the bomb aimer's position.

On that same night Sgt. Lance Holliday, Sgt. Bert Battersby and my old crew were on the same target. Having bombed and set course for home, Geordie called for a four-pound incendiary to be dropped so that he could take a drift. Well, did he have a fire! The little incendiary hit a store of petrol on Benina airport which they were overflying at the time. That four-pounder probably did more damage than the rest of the squadron put together. He didn't get a photograph, but most of us witnessed the conflagration.

When we awoke the following morning we were shown our photograph – the best one we had ever taken, clearly showing ships and even three seaplanes in the harbour, with the cathedral domes visible at the foot of the Cathedral Mole. The photograph was mentioned, but not published, by F.R. Chappell, the Intelligence Officer of 104 Squadron, in his book *Wellington Wings*.

Wingco decided that it was time he took some leave, and that the rest of the crew might go as well. He had friends in

Cairo and opted to stay there, George and I reckoned Palestine to be the place, and I can't remember where the others went. On 8th April I had to prove to the skipper that I could still land in a confined space, and whilst I did a few circuits and bumps he apologised for not allowing me to land more often. I soon found the reason for his anxiety. *'ell for Leather* Z 1045 was due for an engine change and inspection which was to take place at Kabret. En route for Kabret we landed at Helio, where Wingco alighted. His leave had started. We took *'ell* on to Kabret, and started our leave. I've no ideas of its duration now, but it couldn't have been more than twelve days, four of which were spent in travelling. And what travelling! In the back of an old three-ton truck, a 'gharri', we crossed the Suez Canal north of Ismailia, possibly at a place called Kantara, and ground onwards across the Sinai desert where the road was good, but the mountains and wilderness quite cruel. Not a bit of green or drop of moisture anywhere. Not a goat nor a camel, when, after a few hours the gharri stopped for some light relief. In the middle of nowhere we lit up, then, out of nowhere, two Arabs materialised begging cigarettes and selling eggs and tomatoes. We brewed tea and had hard-boiled eggs on the spot, neglecting tomatoes which just had to be washed.

Our fire was the ubiquitous four-gallon petrol can, filled with sand, and saturated with petrol. The Arabs hung around until they realised there was no more baksheesh and melted into the landscape. A few hours after we had restarted our journey we passed El Arish, a small depot on the Mediterranean coast. Somewhere there was a kitbag of mine containing my blue uniforms and woollen under-clothes, pending the time I would be posted to a more temperate zone. We slept the night in the gharri and the following day went through Gaza on our way to Aqir, where we got a lift to Tel Aviv. There we found a nice clean and reasonably cheap pension in which to stay. Our eyes had already looked over much of this beautiful modern city. There was no sign of war, just a few uniforms mingled with what appeared to be a fit and prosperous populace.

We were to learn that many were Palestinian Jews, but most were refugees from Europe and Hitler. Atrocities had taken place, but, at that time in April 1942, no one knew of the genocide which was to come. Most of the houses had brass plates or signs announcing that the house-owners were doctors, dentists, accountants, architects or similar professions. The beautiful sandy beaches were full each day with healthy little children and doting mothers and fathers. The perambulators were small but coachbuilt, like little saloon cars. The hoods were permanent, streamlined and fitted with windows. Many of the people, if not concerned with administration and services, must have worked at the supply depots and NAAFIs. There was a Jewish WVS canteen on the north promenade, where we read books, wrote letters and drank tea, between our visits to the beach and the Richand Kellar. The latter was a real Bavarian beer cellar, near the front, on the main shopping street. We had some of our meals there, and some in the Hollywood Café opposite, a more cosmopolitan place popular with the troops, British, Aussie, New Zealanders, Canadian, Free French, Greek and various allied navy men. The fish and chips and beer were as near to homelike as possible, and Toni, a blonde Jewess, sang alternately, 'Yours til de stahs loos dayer gloreee' and 'Dere vill be blue birts overe, de veit cleefs off Dovere'. After each song her piano accompanist had to be refuelled with a jar or two. Most of the European Jews, and she was one, spoke at least five languages. Russian, German, French, English, Polish, Hebrew, some Italian were all common, with Russian, German and English predominating. At a higher-class restaurant a little further up the road, opposite the opera house, excellent food and wine was served. George and I only afforded it once, and even there we were surprised to find that gherkins, of which I am fond, were charged at tuppence-halfpenny each, on top of service.

On one afternoon we caught a bus to Jaffa, the Arab city south of, but connected to, Tel Aviv. The minarets and mosques, the very antiquity of the place, put one in a different country, the country of crusaders, harems and slave girls. We were advised not to leave the main road which led to the Arab harbour. At roadside kiosks pure Jaffa orange juice, squeezed by press before your very eyes, cost twopence-halfpenny for a half pint. Never did anyone put away more vitamin C but we could not venture too far from the hotel the following day. On our return from Jaffa a very frightening and unnecessary event took place. The bus came upon an Arab funeral, proceeding in the same direction. Scores of people were following the coffin; wailing filled the air. The Jewish bus driver, probably quite innocently, tried to pass the cortège, but was forced to slow almost to a stop. The bus was attacked and hefty Polish soldiers repelled the intending boarders with kicks and punches. The few Arabs riding in the bus were pushed to the floor and kept there whilst the driver, horn blaring, drove through the rioting, stone-throwing mourners. We brave British airmen breathed a sigh of relief when the bus finally got clear and accelerated towards Tel Aviv.

Before our leave finished I had to visit a civilian dentist to have a filling replaced. The plate at the door said 'Dentist', under some Hebrew characters. Since I could not read the name I was surprised to find that an almost blind nurse took me into the lounge of the dentist who was also female, but was sighted at least. The dental chair was in the lounge, where I was fussed over by the two females who, after taking my money, offered me tea and cakes. They were mother and daughter and gave me an invitation to dinner the following day. George said 'Careful Ric,' but he needn't have bothered. During the dinner the new filling fell out, and I wasn't prepared to be operated on that late at night, so said I would return in the morning. I didn't, since we were on our way to Lydda airport where we got a flight to the Canal Zone, then a lift to Kabret, where the RAF dentist made good my tooth. It had been our first leave from the desert of any length, and it spoiled us.

On 23rd April I carried out an air test on 'ell, and with George, Don and Mick, flew it to Heliopolis, where we contacted Wingco and Nick. We were not sorry to be given one more day in Cairo before we all flew back to El Daba on 24th April, to take part in a raid on the following day. I do not recall exactly where the primary target was, I think around Derna or Tobruk, but we could not find it due to bad weather and made for one of the German airfields at Martuba. This time there was no visible damage and we set course to return to base. In crossing the wire we gave our ETA by W/T and George told us we would be first home, since he had been listening out.

As we approached LG 104 we were surprised to see the navigation lights of another aircraft making a wide circuit. We too joined the circuit, to notice that he was given a green Aldis and we a red, to stand by. We circled for a few minutes, waiting for him to land, but he didn't, his lights disappeared and we accepted a green to land. Our navigation lights were on, and we were at 300 feet on the approach, wheels and flaps down, when all hell let loose. Tracer and shell fire smacked into us from astern, and I don't think Mick had time to reply. He could see little anyway with the white navigation light on just above his head. 'JU 88,' he shouted down the intercom as I was leaping into the front turret to man the guns. I shut the doors and cocked the guns, but the intruder had flashed by. Suddenly the ground loomed up and I prayed. I wasn't strapped in and in the panic could not fall back out of the turret. No one, but no one, ever lands in the front turret. Suddenly we thumped the ground and trundled bumpily for a few hundred yards, before stopping in the middle of the aerodrome. Don let me out of his turret and we all hopped through the hatch to survey the damage. Petrol was pouring out onto the ground from a hole in the starboard wing, both main wheel tyres had burst, the tail wheel had broken off, there were holes everywhere, and we only had one elevator. We got as far away from 'ell as possible, in case she went up, or the JU 88 returned. What a lucky escape we had had! Wingco asked if we were all in one piece, and we were surprised to hear Don say he had been hit in two or three places. By way of confirmation he had us inspect his back, where there were several small holes through his Irvin jacket. Protesting, he was stretched out on the ground to await the approaching ambulance, which whisked him to sick quarters and thence to hospital in the Canal Zone. The Wingco's staff car took us to the debriefing tent, where we learned what had happened.

Apparently this unknown aircraft had joined the circuit some ten minutes before we arrived. The Bofors gunners had phoned No. 231 wing, asking for permission to open fire, since they believed it was a bandit. Wing had replied, 'No, get it down, it is a Beaufighter in distress from Malta.' Incredulously the gunners had insisted, but no permission was given. The aerodrome control pilot kept giving the bandit permission to land. It was only when we had been given a green to land that the bandit switched off his navigation lights, got in behind us, and opened fire at close range on the landing approach. The Bofors gunners were watching and opened fire at the enemy, apparently they missed him, but caught us with a friendly 40mm shell in the starboard elevator! We later asked them whose side they were on, and kicked up such a fuss they were given authority to fire at their own discretion on future occasions.

The first 'future occasion' was two days later on 27th April when possibly the same intruder attacked one of our Wimpeys in the circuit, causing it to crash at the Repair and Salvage Unit next door. There was only one survivor. Once again the bandit escaped. We buried those chaps at El Daba, wrapped in blankets. War was very close that day.

Flight Lieutenant Jones came up with an idea to get the intruder, should he pay us another visit. He wanted to rig up a truck with navigation lights fitted on to the end of beams, and mount two twin Lewis gunners in the back. The truck would be stationed a few hundred yards out on the approach to the airfield. When an intruder was reported the truck would switch on its lights, simulating an aircraft, and approach the airfield. The enemy would attack this 'approaching' aircraft, and be shot down by the two ground gunners, who were bouncing about in the back. What the hierarchy thought of the idea I don't know, but it was never put into practice. Within a few days we learned that the intruder had been shot down by Bofors guns near Fuka aerodrome.

On 30th April I collected a new Wellington from Fayoun Road, for Lance Holliday, and to this day I do not know what happened. On landing back at LG 104 I dropped *A for Apple* in from a great height and broke off the tail wheel, giving Mick Navin a nasty bump in the rear turret. My log book refers to it as FP. I can only think that those letters stood for 'FIRST PRANG'.

At this point my tour stood at twenty-two operational sorties, a total of 177 hours. Eight more to go. I was worried that it might take a long time since Wingco was 'rationed' by Group to fly not more than three each month. Then came a shock. Wingco was posted, promoted to Group

Captain of No. 231 Wing which consisted of two Wellington squadrons, 37 and 70 Squadrons.

In June I was to get in thirteen more operations, mostly with a Canadian Sergeant Habeshaw. The situation must have been desperate. They wouldn't let me be 'tour expired'. It was the month when the cards foretold I should be wounded. I must say that things were so warm, it could have happened at any time. But it didn't and I don't believe in fortune telling to this day.

We celebrated Wingco's promotion with a huge party in the well-dug-in Sergeants' Mess. We just sat around as crews, sang the usual songs and did the usual 'turns'.

> Now this old shirt of mine,
> has had its. . . . time:
> Roll on the good ship Taura Peachy,
> So fling it far and wide;
> Roll on the good ship Taura Peachy.

Having gone through the vest, shorts, pants, shoes and socks, the singer would be starkers, and soon bathed in beer. The old hands with multi-year Indian tours usually performed that one.

I went indoors like a nice girl should
and he followed me like I hoped he would.
That handsome airman whomever he may be,
listen and I'll tell you what he did to me.
I went upstairs like a nice girl should,
and he followed me like I knew he would.
That handsome airman whomever he may be,
listen and I'll tell you what he did to me.
I put on my nightie like a nice girl should,
and he took it off like I knew he would.
That handsome airman whomever he may be,

listen and I'll tell you what he did to me.
I got into bed like a nice girl should,
and he followed me like I hoped he would.
That handsome airman whomever he may be,
it's none of your bloody business what he did to me.

Usually sung heartily by the whole squadron, when in their cups.

Just a little bit of heaven fell from out the sky one
        day,
and it nestled in the ocean not so very far away,
but when the Air Force saw it why it looked so bloody
        bare,
they said that's what we're looking for,
we'll send our Air Force there.
So they sent out river gun boats,
armoured cars and SHQ,
and they sent the fighting seventieth out in the
        bleedin' blue,
but peachy we'll be going to a land that's far remote,
but until then, all I can say's
'Roll on that. . . . boat!'
I've got those Shaibah blues,
Shai – ai – bah blues,
I'm fed up and I'm choked up and I'm blue,
I've tried to learn the lingo, but it really gets my goat,
the only thing that I can say's
'Roll on that. . . . boat',
I've got those Shaibah blues,
Shai – ai – bah blues,
I'm fed up and I'm choked up and I'm blue,

Shaibah, where it was I didn't care. Little did I realise that I'd find out long before my war was over.

79

The party was drawing to a close. Our wireless op, Oscar George Ackerman, presented Wingco with a large soup ladle – it must have held one third of a pint. It was filled with whisky and 'Wingco' (now 'Groupy') downed it. An argument started and the flight lieutenant commanding officer of the neighbouring RSU lunged at our skipper. Oscar George dived across the table, rugger tackled the Flight Looey, and we all sat on him. The crew smuggled O.G. out into the sandstorm. Outside the air was stifling and full of dust. Visibility was nil, and not improved by my night blindness. I staggered towards my tent, but after an interminable age I collided with a Wellington. I must have wandered in a circle, and, totally lost, I camped under the tailplane for the night. Towards dawn the wind dropped, and the air cleared. My sweaty bod and KD were covered in dust, so, by first light I was in the Med, uniform and all. Much refreshed and dripping I was first on breakfast parade. Back at our tent the others had not missed me. With Wingco gone, I worried about my future. Wing Commander Woods was not too pleased with my flying, and he didn't hug the 'ops' as my former skipper had. I would be there for ever. Seven months had gone. I was not on my way home, wounded.

5th June 1942 saw me teamed up with Sgt. Thomas, my twenty-third operation of the thirty which I had to collect to complete my tour. Then I was crewed with a Canadian, a Sgt. Habeshaw. We bombed Benghasi, Herakleon in Crete twice with success, and on 12th June 1942 we set out to bomb shipping in Benghasi harbour. Rommel was receiving his major reinforcements through that port. This was to be number twenty-seven. Four to go.

The outward flight in Wellington *D for Donald* was uneventful, and Wingco's crew was beginning to work with this Canadian sergeant. Our bombing run was from the sea in a southerly direction. Searchlights were very active and

80

ack-ack more concentrated than usual. Our target, from 11,000 feet was the Juliana Mole. 'Bomb doors open; left, left ------steady.' Then it happened. Searchlights picked us up. Exploding shells buffeted us. Our driver was disorientated in the searchlights. Whether we stalled or whether a shell tipped a wing, I don't know. *D for Donald* was streaking earthwards vertically. The altimeter was unwinding at a lick. The air speed indicator was off the clock, and the clock could read up to 320 mph, 50 mph past our limiting speed. 'Jettison the bombs,' I yelled as I heaved on the control column with Habeshaw. The searchlights went out as we screamed earthwards. Habeshaw had closed the bomb doors. Oscar George went past me, parachute at the ready. Somehow I grabbed his belt with one hand and persuaded him to stay. We closed the throttles, stick fully back and after a long hesitation *D* responded. On these occasions the altimeter lags. At the bottom of the dive it read 1500; we were a great deal lower.

Pulling out of the dive we sailed back up to 9000 feet with full boost added, and she would not level out until we stalled at the top. 'Home James.' The shakiest do I had experienced. With boost at 'plus two', *D* vibrated her way homewards at 105 mph Skipper was shaken and shaking. The controls were vibrating badly. Controls had been badly strained but slowly, and losing height, we made it over the wire three hours after leaving the target area. Landing ground number 117, near Fuka, hove into sight. Circling we signalled for the chance light for landing. Downwind, wheels down, across wind, into wind, flaps down. The chance light was slowly approaching, but a half mile short the wheels hit the ground. With brakes full on and switches cut, *D* quickly came to a halt, a long way from the landing ground.

On tumbling out of the hatch we found that we had stopped on a hill between a pile of stones and a slit trench. The chance light was still roaring flat out and illuminating the airfield. It was not extinguished until we turned all our lights out. By daylight we inspected *D* to find that we had lost acres of canvas and the elevator roller hinges had been spread, causing the elevators to flutter in the turbulence. Leaving *D* there we were collected by another aircraft. The entry in my log book has 'R.S.D.' annotated alongside. It must mean 'Real Shaky Do'. At 70 Squadron's seventieth anniversary dinner at Lyneham in 1986, I met Vic Adkins, a ground gunner at LG 117 who witnessed the incident at Fuka.

Two days, or rather two nights later, we were on our way back to Benghasi, and at this time I wrote 'N.T.A.A.', No Trouble At All. Number twenty-eight . . . two to go.

Train after train had been travelling up to the front in Cyrenaica, and each one was loaded with tanks. We could see the railway south of our airfield and we knew something was brewing. An offensive was not far off.

It must have been mid-June when General Ritchie had his 300 tanks lured into a dried-up wadi where they were blasted by 88mm anti-tank guns and Tiger tanks. On 16th June I bombed Timimi and hit a pyrotechnic and ammunition store. Number twenty-nine. On the 18th it was back to Benghasi again, and on the 22nd back to Timimi. That made thirty-one. No hope now of going home, the army was in full retreat. 24th June was Benghasi again, and after that the Desert Rats were streaking down the desert road, heading due east. For five days the trucks passed, some towing others. There were no tanks and few guns in the rout. Jerry had thrashed us, and we were all shamed. Almost the last vehicle to pass was a huge grader towing a line of broken-down trucks, loaded with exhausted Tommies.

By 26th June Jerry had reached the Sidi Barrani, Mersa Matruh area. We were given *carte blanche* to find them and bomb them. I felt no remorse as we blasted their tanks and trucks and troop concentrations. They did not fire back as we strafed. We fetched a new *D for Donald* from Cairo West on 28th June, Jerry had got to Fuka, and we found him after twenty minutes flying. Three sorties we made that night, bombing Rommel's vanguard but having no appreciable effect. Jerry was but thirty miles from LG 104 as we loaded up and took off with our personal possessions for LG 224, Cairo West. Our few vehicles were loaded up with spares and ground equipment. Our bomb dump was blown up. Airborne, I looked back to see the wreck of old *'ell for Leather* on her knees in a corner of the landing ground. Surely we had not lost. All of 70 Squadron were alive to fight another day. Ritchie was fired, but his successor was killed in a Bombay crash.

The story got to us about the officer in charge of our ground gunners. When we left LG 104, Flt. Lt. Jones, ancient, white-haired, and courageous, remained behind, intending to delay the Bosch tanks with his Lewis gunners! He disobeyed his orders to drive east. The army were sent to fetch him and he was loath to leave. His gunners were less unhappy to go, with the Tiger tanks but ten minutes away.

We bombed Mersa from Cairo West, now a five hour round trip, and from our new base at Abu Suier we hit Fuka, overflying LG 104, now occupied by the Luftwaffe. We were sorely tempted to unload there in error. We need not have bothered. On 2nd July, in *N for Nuts* we bombed hell out of LG 104, to orders.

Short of aircraft and of crews I was asked by Squadron Leader Stanbury to air-test *H for Harry*, our training Wimpey, to ascertain whether she would be fit for service. There was a slender moon as I took off at about 21.30. She was very noisy, needed a lot of nursing, but the air-test was otherwise uneventful. She had a full fuel load but no bombs. I landed back at Abu Suier, bounced a bit, and was told by Stan to take her round again. Willingly I lined up, opened the throttles and lumbered down the runway. Slowly the speed built up 60, 70, 80 mph Then, almost running out of runway she began to slow. Nothing for it. At 70 mph, out of runway, I yanked her into the air, pulling up the undercart as she rose. With engines flat out, on full boost, she staggered along about fifty feet off the ground. The speed would not increase so a turn or a climb was out of the question. What to do? I cannot remember now when I first noticed it, but the flap indicator showed full flaps! The selector was in mid position and I cursed a faulty valve. I was glad the Nile Delta was flat, yet there it was! The tallest tree in Egypt was dead ahead. I dare not turn, so when a collision seemed unavoidable I eased *H* skywards, shutting my eyes.

We missed, I opened my eyes, the airspeed was now 60 mph. I prayed. The answer seemed to be to take off the flap, little by little. When you are on your own in a Wimpey, absolutely petrified, and but one hundred feet up, you need some luck. I didn't get any. A flick upwards with the flap selector and none came off. Another flick – nothing. Damn it, what next? I put the lever up and left it so, concentrating on making a wide 60 mph sweep to try and reach the runway. It was two miles south. Suddenly it happened. Now every Wimpey pilot knows that the kite falls between two and three hundred feet when full flap comes off. As I struggled to keep the engines going and wings level, that is exactly what happened, only I didn't have two hundred feet to fall. I felt her go and heaved back on the control column. She thumped into the desert tail first and skated along her belly.

She stopped. Amazed, I was alive, unhurt. Then flames licked out of the starboard engine, and I was doing a forward dive out of the cockpit roof fully eight feet to the ground, where I arrived unhurt. From a few yards I watched *H* burn, thankful that I had been alone. Those few yards turned into several hundred when the ammo, which I had forgotten, started to explode. She was a pyre; almost mine. Then I saw a pair of headlamps approaching from the east, and ran towards the jeep. The army had rescued me. They were relieved to know that no one else was aboard, and drove me back to Abu Suier sick quarters via their camp.

As we drove away I saw many lights approaching from the aerodrome to the south, and the medical officer was surprised to see me in one piece. I felt fine. 'Have a cigarette,' he said. I held out my hand for the fag, but it was shaking too much. The MO lit the thing and stuck it in my mouth. About twenty minutes later the phone rang, and the MO beckoned me to take the receiver. It was Squadron Leader Stanbury, saying he had returned from the crash and there was no sign of Sgt. Barfoot. 'The poor bugger's had it.' He couldn't believe that it was hysterical laughter he was hearing. A visit next day to the site of the crash found only the engines were recognisable. The aluminium had run away from the site in rivers of molten metal.

I smoked a lot of Victory Vs that night. They were the free issue made from camel dung. Every airman was given one hundred a week. They were usually spotted with green mould. Our squadron MO had forbidden us to smoke them, and we usually fed them, packets and all, to two small deer which the squadron had acquired. The deer thrived. I told Stan that *H* had lost power and that the engines had cut. The only lie I was ever proud of.

Eddie Lomas was posted home and on my sister's birthday, 4th July, the night after my prang, I was entrusted with his Wimpey, *B for Bertie*. With a new crew we set off to bomb Daba, and to strafe Jerry. All went well, but as we went in to assist an American Liberator strafing the coast road, the Lib opened fire on us, as it made off at a rate of knots. Whether it was the Lib or the enemy, I don't know. The return to Abu Suier found us brakeless and *B for Bertie* shot off the end of the runway and ended up a mile further on in an irrigation ditch with her back broken. I thanked the crew for getting me out, as I came round to find the MO putting stitches in my forehead. They swore that I opened the hatch and dived out with a forward roll in a split second, and showed the rest the way. Practice makes perfect I suppose. Sgt. McKay, I'm sorry to say, had to have stitches in his nose, but that was the only hurt I ever inflicted on one of our own side, so far as I'm aware.

On the very next day I was visited by Oscar George Ackerman, who had been reposted to 104 Squadron from the transit camp, whence he was due home. On his first trip with 104 Squadron his aircraft had been shot down, and he had bailed out, meeting an army patrol after three days. He was finally on his way home, a qualified 'Caterpillar'.

I was also deemed to have finished my tour, at great expense to the allied cause. One Wimpey bent, one strained beyond repair; shot down once and crashed twice. I did not accept the title 'Pranger' with any enthusiasm. Some unkind aircrew hinted that, left alive, I was much more helpful to the German war effort, and that Hitler had ordered my preservation. Whatever the truth I found myself posted to Ferry Flight at Fayid by 16th July 1942.

Fayid, a brand new aerodrome near Kasfareet on the Great Bitter Lake, had not been officially opened and we were the first lonely unit to occupy it. 'We' were Flt. Sgt. Mickey Vertican, a regular airframe fitter turned pilot, Bob Mann, Harry Dawson and yours truly, all on rest, ex 70 Squadron. Mick was the only SNCO commanding officer that I ever met or served under. He had finished his tour on 148 Squadron, Merlin-engined Wellingtons. Much later on Halifaxes he was to carry on to bomb northern Italy with two engines out, ditch in the Med and float around for many days before rescue. A DFC, a CGM, and a commission in the field were then to be his lot. At a reunion in the 1980s I discovered that he retired as a very long-serving officer in 1964. He never wanted to be commissioned anyway. I never did find out how he collected his broken nose.

Ensconced in new billets, bug-free, we four pilots with a flight sergeant fitter and a few ground crew shared a new mess. We were given one Wellington Ic, Z8734 as a taxi. We became a collection and delivery mob scouring the Middle East and western desert, rescuing old and new, serviceable and damaged kites. We each collected several, and I left my silver cigarette case in one of them.

We made several trips to Luxor, where I bought a genuine Greek coin and a holy Scarab for two piastres (5d). Whilst on a collection trip to Fayoun Road I met Pilot Officer Crerar, who had just landed a Beaufighter. He looked the part and showed genuine pleasure at the meeting, if only because I was flying a lumbering pig of a plane. I had last seen him at No. 5 ITW in Paignton, where he had beaten me in a cross country race.

Our aerodrome was officially opened in early August 1942, when an advanced guard of the USAAF arrived in two massive Liberators. We were very apologetic when we invited the crews to tiffin, where they shared our bully beef, raw onions, weevil-infested bread, margarine, tomatoes, dates and marmalade. We couldn't muster enough beer for a bottle each. If they were shattered by the available rations they didn't show it, but between two doorsteps they sloshed all the rest of the victuals. The only bully beef, date and marmalade sandwiches I have seen.

No. 4 MIDDLE EAST
TRAINING SCHOOL, KABRET

On 31st August 1942 Mick Vertican flew Bob, Harry and me the few miles to Kabret, where we found ourselves absorbed into a new unit. No. 4 Middle East Training School. Mick Vertican flew off and we never saw him again. Kabret was to be the school training the Long Range Desert Group in parachute jumping. Army parachute instructors included Warrant Officer Dawes, a veteran of one hundred jumps at Ringway, and a Scottish sergeant, whose name eludes me. I was to meet him two years later in Italy, where I dropped him often into Yugoslavia. Jerry was knocking at the gates of Alex and the unit explored the possibility of a move to Rosh Pinnar in Northern Palestine.

We dropped the paratroops in training for day after day. Sometimes as a display before staff brown jobs. Sometimes on target, sometimes in the drink. Mine had to hurl themselves down through a well, aft of the Elsan in a Wellington Ic. Harry and Bob converted to flying our Hudson. Harry broke the Hudson. The commanding officer was Flight Lieutenant C. Wright, a grand fellow, known as 'Wilbur'. He was later to shoot down an Me 110 with his one machine gun in the nose of his Hudson, as he broke the Malta blockade. The story went like this: Wilbur was a few miles short of Malta when he espied this Me 110 creeping up behind his Hudson. As soon as the 110 opened fire with its cannon, Wilbur selected flaps down, shot up a few hundred feet, whilst the 110 slipped past below. With that it was 'flaps off' and Wilbur dropped in behind the 110 with his peashooter blasting. The 110 ended up in the drink. Wilbur got the DFC.

Rommel was a short drive from Alexandria and the shopkeepers and hoteliers were looking forward to a change of patrons. King Farouk was sure that he would soon be entertaining German VIPs and it took the British Ambassador and some tanks to dissuade him from active co-operation. It was strongly rumoured that he and his yacht were then blockaded in Lake Timsah.

Rommel launched his delayed attack on the night of 30th/31st August with the full strength of the Afrika Korps. The Panzers ran into our anti-tank defences and by the evening of 31st August 1942 they retired badly dented to the Ragil Depression where the advance, Rommel's last throw, was halted and defeated by the Army gunners, the RAF, the SAAF, and the newly arrived USAAF.

On the night of 23rd October 1942, two Long Range Desert Group gunners, together with a Breda 88mm anti-tank/anti-aircraft gun, took off from Kabret. We knew neither reason nor destination. After 2200 hours the radio informed all that a massive Allied barrage had opened up on the luckless Afrika Korps, at El Alamein. Seventy bombers switched their targets from Axis airfields and roads to troop positions. In the early hours the Wimpey returned with a huge hole blasted in its side, and both LRDG men wounded. The 88mm had been jettisoned. The kite was a wreck – a tribute to the strength of the Wellington that she had returned at all. It later transpired that these two commandos were to have been dropped on the German side of an Afrika Korps minefield, together with their gun. They were to have opened fire on the enemy tanks in full retreat through a minefield gap. The story went that whilst running in for the drop, the Wimpey was hit by a Panzer tank gun!

Within days our prisoner of war cages were filling and we were using Italian prisoners as labourers. A refusal to dig was met by the withdrawal of water. They dug! The Afrika Korps had overstretched their supply lines. Egyptians realised they would not be handling marks, and the air was scented with victory at last. A little ashamedly, Bob, Harry and I did not regret that we were resting.

Days passed in giving air experience, day and night parachute drops, and duties as aerodrome control pilot. Harry, Bob and I spent our off duty hours in the Salvation Army canteen or in Shafto's, the open-air, prone-to-break-down cinema.

On 2nd October 1942, I flew Wimp AD 639, with Sgt. Ray Embury, our Aussie navigator, to Aqir, I knew not why. I guess it was to pick up Bob and Harry who had delivered a kite to the Maintenance Unit. Somehow they had collected six passengers who required a lift to Egypt. One was a uniformed nurse, who sat in the co-pilot's seat, suspended over the bomb aimer's position. As we flew we gradually overtook another Wimp on the same course, and in passing I sounded the undercarriage warning horn, by pressing the test button. 'I didn't know aircraft had horns,' she said, and Bob and Harry guffawed from the bomb aimer's position. We arrived safely, and our passengers left for the Officers' Mess. Bob and Harry remarked that the nurse had lovely legs, which they had admired from below for one hour and thirty-five minutes, less the take-off and landing times.

Once every four or five nights one of us had to act as aerodrome control pilot, and sleep in lonely isolation in the watchtower on the airfield, pending an emergency. During November I took up my bed and established myself in the tower. It began to rain and rain and rain. I was in for a quiet night. In the early hours I was awakened by the landline telephone. 'Fayid airfield is out, prepare to receive two Halifaxes.' Hell! Groundsheet on, I drove through the streaming rain to the pit at the intersection of the runway to await the sound of the aircraft overhead, and to switch on the modern electric flarepath. The rain teemed down and ran into the pit. Within a few minutes I heard first one and then the second four-engined aircraft. I engaged the switches and the runways were illuminated. I flashed a green to Halifax number one. The whole runway system shorted, fused and darkness reigned. The runway lights were not proof against rain and flood. What to do? A dash back to the tower to collect a few goose-necks, and a frantic attempt to light them with a soggy box of Egyptian matches. Match after match fizzled out, until with three left I managed to light one paraffin wick. Meanwhile the Halibags, puzzled, circled and circled. With the flaring goose-neck I lit two more and placed them at 100 yard intervals on the port side of the runway. I had no more, so with fingers crossed I again flashed my green Aldis. Number one approached, still in pouring rain, with landing lights full on. He made a super touchdown and drifted safely off the runway to let in number two, who landed safely but more heavily. Two Halifaxes saved by Barfoot and three paraffin flares. What commendation or award awaited me? An irate wigging from both exhausted crews left me disillusioned. 'Why,' I asked, 'was Fayid unable to receive them?' 'Because their flarepath had fused in the torrential rain,' they replied.

On 19th December 1942 our one Wellington DV 677 fell due for a 240-hour inspection. We were granted leave together to Palestine to await the completion and we spent a glorious eleven days in Tel Aviv, where the Jewish WVS had a quiet club for the entertainment and refreshment of Allied soldiery. Here we were to meet a Mrs Mondry, a well-educated lady who spoke a multitude of languages. We were such good-looking, clean-living boys that she invited us home where we were to meet her two nieces. Bob was out – he was married. We were surprised to find Mrs Mondry reading Tolstoy's *War and Peace*, whilst awaiting us, and her nieces. The nieces came, two sweet girls. One was thirteen and the other fourteen. The thirteen-year-old was named Ruth. The other I forget.

Just before Christmas Day we went to Jerusalem and visited the Church of all Nations, in the Garden of Gethsemane, the Church of Nativity in Bethlehem, the Wailing Wall of the old temple and what could have been the Holy Sepulchre. Jerusalem even then was commercialised and full of Arabs selling souvenirs to Christians. I bought presents to send home, and my wife still has her pyjamas and kimono, her mother-of-pearl-covered New Testament and her olive leaf from the Garden of Gethsemane. On Christmas Day at 10.30 am, Bob, Harry and I attended the service in the courtyard of the Church of Holy Nativity. The bells of Bethlehem were clanging out, each in its own little tower. At 11 am the bells were broadcast to home and to the world, as was the service which we attended. Each of us sang 'Christians Awake' with gusto, as if to hope we could send our love home thereby. It was a most moving morning, one I would never have missed, but one I could never repeat.

Back in Tel Aviv, the fleshpots of the battle zone, good living caused toothaches yet again. A Russian dentist was recommended. His sitting room was his surgery, and our common language was German. Between the '*Schmerz?*' and the '*Nein*' he fixed my teeth, ripping out old fillings and fixing up my mouth well enough to see the war out. He had been a dentist to the Czar, I learned, and certainly I could have been royalty. He was gentle. Mouth completed I parted with two Palestinian pounds, and was immediately invited to drink it back at his seventieth birthday party on the following day. This I gladly did and met some delightful people, most of whom spoke five or six languages, including

English. However I only met one Palestinian Jew in the RAF. He was the airman of the watch at LG 104. and he taught me to make Russian tea in a fifty-cigarette tin, over three candles or a hurricane lamp. The idea was to make a very strong tea syrup, to which boiling water was added. When I asked the fit young men of Tel Aviv whether they wouldn't relish the chance to take on the Wehrmacht, the reply always contained 'Have we not suffered enough!' Certainly most of them were refugees.

Between Christmas Day and New Year's Eve, I spent an evening at the Hollywood Café, sitting alone and imbibing a beer or two. Suddenly there came a thump round the ear, and I was looking up at a giant Aussie, who was soon apologising. 'Sorry Cobber, didn't know you were a Pommie. Thought you was a Yank.' Apparently they had once been bombed by the Stars and Stripes, in error. From then on I was obliged to quaff whatever alcohol the Digger and his two friends put before me. It was well after midnight when, having exchanged photographs, they hoisted me on to an acquired auto-cycle and pushed me down the road to the promenade. Out of range I dismounted by falling off and hurried to my pension. On New Years' Day 1943 we collected DN 677 from the maintenance unit at Aqir and returned to base.

On 26th January 1943, Harry and I, with an LAC engine-fitter, were flown in a Hudson to Gambut No. 3 landing ground, together with tent, rations and bed rolls, to collect our Wellington DV 677 which had been on an LRDG mission, but had forced-landed. The airfield was deserted, and the Hudson flew off, leaving us to inspect the Wimp. The port motor was OK on run-up, but one magneto on the starboard motor was totally u/s, and the other unreliable. What to do? There was no way we could make contact with base, and take-off was out of the question. We explored the landing ground, finding lots of German and Italian garbage.

On one dump the airman found some scrap German dry batteries, the centre pole of which was a solid stick of carbon. We needed magneto brushes, didn't we? So we sat down to whittle and file down these sticks of carbon to a diameter of about one eighth of an inch, and approximately half an inch in length. I was hopeless. The more I tried the more ham fisted I became and the carbon fractured.

Finally, after three days, Harry had made one and the fitter, our saviour, made three. Brushes fitted, I warily tried the engines as Harry and the airman took turns in cranking. Pessimism disappeared as the engine burst into life and elation took over as the magneto drops were within bounds. We could fly out, and this we did on 1st February 1943. Apprehension dissipated as the flight progressed and we made a safe landing, only to find that I had been posted. To Blighty some eight months late? Not on your Nelly! To Paiforce at Habbaniya. I'd never heard of it, but enquiries elicited that it was situated in Iraq. The then CO of No. 4 METS, a squadron leader, whose signature I cannot decipher, assessed me as an average paratroop dropper and was gracious to certify my 682 hours. This officer had been overheard in Shepherds, Cairo, to recall how, on a Whitley raid over Milan, enemy action had deprived him of two and a half fingers. His audience, two USAAF officers' sympathised, not knowing that his fingers had been lost whilst rolling a jeep!

A REST!

As I recall, Harry was the first to be notified of his posting and he left the unit before I did. I think my journey started with an uncomfortable truck ride across the Sinai peninsula, through Gaza, to Haifa. It must have taken two days at least. Then I transferred to a small-gauge mountain railway for the next stage to Damascus. St Paul must have had a much more uncomfortable journey in his day, as mine was on wooden slatted seats. My rations for the journey were a loaf of bread and a tin of sardines. The tin had no key, and I had lost my clasp knife with two blades, a tin opener and a thing for untying knots and getting stones out of horses' hooves. At one point along the hilly route the train puffed more slowly than the children running alongside the track. It was here I struck a bargain. My tin of sardines for a sandbag full of grapefruit. What luxury! I ate five, was uncomfortable for the rest of the journey and arrived in Damascus in a perilous state of insecure queasiness. Recovery came without accident or embarrassment and I saw the film *The Midas Touch*, in English, at a Syrian cinema. On the following day, whilst awaiting my onwards transmission, I visited a small glassworks, where beer bottles by the thousand were poured into the furnace, and glass blowers made everything from vases to oil lamp glasses. The next visit was to another small factory where cloth was handwoven. In one dark alcove, a man and boy operated a large hand loom. They threw shuttles to each other as the warps divided; or was it the wefts? The brocade was beautiful, with silver and many coloured threads in a close pattern. It was two pounds a metre, and I only had thirty bob, so three-quarters of a metre it had to be. Now, sixty years later, my wife is still trying to decide what to make with three-quarters of a metre of silver silk brocade from Damascus! I carried that brocade, together with twelve metres of white crêpe de Chine for at least the next two years. The crêpe I had bought some time in Cairo for Kitty's wedding dress.

It was about this time that my expectation to 'buy it' gradually changed to a determination to survive and see the war through. That determination was to be dented from time to time.

It was a Sunday afternoon when I caught the Nairn Transporter for my 600 mile trip across the desert to Habbaniya. The Nairn Transport Company had started on this roadless route, Damascus to Baghdad, in 1919, two Aussies with two lorries. They now had huge trucks and trans-desert buses, much wider than the norm and each carrying two drivers. One huge, ten-foot wide, double-decker coach towed a double-decker trailer of equal size, and these leviathans hurtled across the roadless desert at sixty miles an hour, following the oil pipeline route. The huge headlights lit up the desert, where there was but sand to see, until the stop at H 3, an oil pipeline pumping station, for refreshments.

Journey completed, I arrived at Habbaniya, the second largest Royal Air Force station in the world (the largest by then since Changi had fallen to the Japs), where I reported to the Commanding Officer of Communications Flight, Pai-force (Persia and Iraq Forces). The CO was Squadron Leader Lenton, and I was detailed to B Flight, whose commander was a Flight Lieutenant Humphries. On this flight I found my old pal Harry, who had been re-posted since leaving No. 4 METS. Harry and I shared an airy room equipped with a ceiling fan, beds of the tubular hospital kind and real mattresses. We were issued with two sheets, one of which was exchanged each week. Real sheets! What luxury. The camp was a small town in its own right. It had riding stables, shops, bazaars, its own cattle farm, hospital, and indoor and outdoor swimming pools. The one disadvantage? Bullsh... ruled. Our SNCO's mess was one of three. All of Comm. Flight's dozen pilots messed there, as did the SNCOs of the maintenance unit, and its one test pilot, a sixty-year-old Pole by the name of Schulzewski. He was bald and fat, a superb pilot who had flown one hundred types of aircraft. He only admitted to fifty years and accepted his new name of 'Soda Whisky'.

Opposite Comm. Flight's crew room was a little hut on stilts which had been turned into a quaint little NAAFI canteen. One day we were imbibing tea and nattering. Flight Lieutenant Humphries was telling us that he was a well-known actor, pre-war. I had to admit he was pretty suave. Like an idiot I asked what films he had starred in. All were unknown to me until he mentioned *The Midas Touch*. Oh, I'd seen that in Damascus, but I hadn't noticed him. 'What part did you play?' Embarrassed, he replied, 'The policeman.' Now I remembered. He had had to say, 'Where's your licence?' Somehow I don't think we were the best of friends thereafter.

Here, when not flying, we played bridge. In the hot season when temperatures hit 125° F in the shade, we worked from 6 am until 1 pm and then rested it off on the charp. We had, as a communications flight, fourteen aircraft I think. Three venerable twin-engined Valentia troop transports, two Airspeed Oxfords, two Gladiators, an Audax, a Hart, a Wellesley, a Fairchild, a Bombay, a short-nosed Blenheim, a Gypsy Moth and a DH Rapide. Of these I flew the Valentia, Oxford, Gladiator, Audax, Wellesley, Bombay and Gypsy Moth as pilot, and the rest as co-pilot. Life was more leisurely and restful, though not without incident.

After three days I was dropping parachutists of the Assyrian Levies, whose families lived in the civilian cantonment, from a Valentia. This was a huge biplane, with twin, wooden four-bladed propellers. It had a biplane tail with three fins like a box kite, a fixed undercarriage of four wheels, and the revolution counters could only be read from dials on the engines, if visibility was good. The pilots sat on top of the whale-like body in the open air, and the artificial horizon was an adjustable wire stretched horizontally between two masts in front of the windshield. A vertical tube half-filled with a coloured liquid indicated the position of the nose, and the 'modern' turn and bank indicator made one glad that clouds were few and could be avoided. These Valentias, late of 70 Squadron, had been used as bombers against the army of Raschid Ali in 1941–42, as had the Oxfords. The Gladiators were the survivors of those which had downed a couple of Me 110s trying to take off at Baghdad airport. We used them for meteorological climbs at 6 am each day. As a boy I had always wanted to fly a Gloster Gladiator, my favourite, the height of my ambition. It did not disappoint me. It had six 0.303 machine guns, cruised at 165 mph, was most manoeuvrable and a joy to aerobat. At 6.30 am, at 24,000 feet, with oxygen on, the world was one's oyster.

The Oxfords and the Wellesley were used to carry staff VIPs, the Audax to tow targets for the Army Bofors gun school. Flights were usually short, but few days went by without a trip somewhere in something. Assyrian Levy paratroops were trained and retrained but they could never be dropped in a very short stick. Each man insisted on crossing himself before dropping through the hole in the floor! During the second half of February, 1943, I transported senior officers to and between Basra, Abadan and Baghdad. The climate was cool and pleasant, almost icy cold at night. During early March I converted a Canadian, W/O Marshall; a Yank, Sgt. Wood; and an Aussie, Sgt. Campey, to fly the Valentia and the Oxford.

10th March saw Sgt. Campey and I set out for Ur of the Chaldeas, in Valentia 1311. I can't remember why but there was a railhead and an army transit camp at Ur. There was evidence of pre-war archaeological digging, and rumours of a nomadic tribe of non-Christians who nevertheless had crosses tattooed on the backs of their hands. They were reputed to be inhospitable in the extreme, and wizards with sharp knives. That day we made Shaibah, famed for the 'Shaibah Blues', that 'little bit of heaven that fell out the skies one day'. Here I found the camp padre to be S/Ldr. the Rev. P. Johnston, curate at my home town when I had left, and assistant scoutmaster of our Sixth St Leonards Scout Troop.

From Shaibah we made a return trip to Ur on the 11th, and another on 12th March. The desert was so flat that we taxied almost the whole way back to Shaibah from Ur, just lifting over camel thorn now and again. It relieved the boredom but was quite idiotic. Suffice it to say that the Valentia took off at fifty, flew at eighty and landed at fifty miles per hour. As it taxied at eighty we lost no time. I'm sure Campey did not approve.

On 28th March Harry and I, in Valentia 3600, set out for the lower slopes of the mountains south-west of Teheran to look for an Indian army signals unit which had been cut off by floods as it erected a signals line, and had run out of food. The camp was near a village called Badra, and we chugged around the sky for fully half an hour before we spotted a smoke column. There they were, waving like mad.

I throttled back to 45 mph and descended to fifty feet, since it was to be a dead drop of rice in sacks. The first sack hit the dropping zone and burst. The second hit the dropping zone and burst. What to do? Just over the track, the other side of the telephone wires was a short level piece of ground and I decided to have a go at landing with the rest of the load. The Valentia dragged herself over the wires at 45 mph, hanging on the props, and flopped on to the earth. Full inefficient brakes stopped her, her nose over a gulley! Indians towed her back to the track where we unloaded the rice and other supplies and helped the officer drink some of the teetotal Sikhs' rations of beer. Useful liaison justified the risk.

Came the time to leave, and we had to take turns in pumping up a pressurised tank before releasing this compressed air into the engine cylinders as a self-starter. Finally. after pumping for what seemed like hours, we got one engine going. When we were desperate our fitter foraged in the fuselage and brought out a long rope with a strong canvas bag fitted to one end. The idea was to slip the bag over the end of a prop blade, and for a six-man team to haul on the rope, to turn the prop, and hopefully to start the engine. With two teams sprawled in the dust, a reluctant third team started the rogue engine and hopes rose. Now I reckon we had 120 yards of flat between the telephone wires and the ditch so, tail under the wires, I opened the throttles wide on the brakes, pushed the stick forward with Harry's help, and released the brakes. *Three Six Double O* lumbered forward, the gulley approached, and, not daring to look at the airspeed, I eased the stick back before the wheels reached the ditch. Luckily the ground fell away and, empty now, we soared, Airborne! Another life!

We circled, waved, and made for Baghdad to refuel, before returning to base. Without special overloads the Val had a range of five hours at eighty miles per hour. However into a headwind if you were not half-way in two and a half hours, then you turned back to return in very quick time.

Against a 40 mph wind our groundspeed was but 40 mph but turn around and she sped along at a full 120 mph. The huge wing area meant that the Val could carry almost all one could stuff into her, but on the ground in a high wind, she had to be tethered, lest she took off by herself! Just like a huge kite. Our experience on that dead drop was well worth it, because we discovered that a sack of rice, put in another loose sack, meant that it was possible to drop any amount without loss. The inner sack burst but the outer one kept the rice together. I wonder if there are records of earlier supply drops, without the use of parachutes?

There were very good sports facilities at Habbaniya, and we enjoyed games of tennis on hard courts in the cooler early spring. Irrigation ditches ensured that flowers could be grown in profusion by the Iraqi gardeners. Leaving the court one day I passed some glorious sweet peas and picked a small bunch with which to adorn our room. Contentedly I strolled back to the mess for four o'clock chai and wads. Suddenly, a weight landed on my back, and simultaneously a hairy arm reached past my right ear and grabbed the flower heads. My attacker jumped down, eating my bouquet as it fled. I was quite amazed to see a medium-sized ape, and I discovered, in telling my story at the mess, that it lived in each of the three SNCOs' messes in turn. It shunned the officers' food. I was later to watch it on many evenings amble from sleepy mess member to sleepy mess member, swigging the Canadian Black Label from the bottles on side tables and on the floor. It played the piano with hands and feet, and entertained us all by swinging between the rafters. Even when four sheets to the wind, totally Harry Liszt, it would swing across the room. When it missed it was pissed, but it tried again and again.

1st April 1943 was the 25th anniversary of the formation of the Royal Air Force, April Fool's Day, 1918. Paiforce Communications Flight was to put on an air display at

Baghdad airport, in the presence of Young King Faisal. Sgt. Chapman was duty pilot at Baghdad control tower, and he and some airmen were sprucing the place up on the morning of 1st April. Suddenly he espied a well-dressed Arab slinking round the deserted airport buildings. Now Chapman was a big fellow and his instructions, in view of the Royal visit, were to keep the airport secure. This he did by grabbing the intruder by collar and crutch, and propelling him down the steps into the road outside.

After tiffin the assorted aircraft of Comm. Flight were flown the sixty miles to Baghdad. Harry and I took the Oxford. She had a warped tail but could be trimmed OK for flight. Landing was a bit fraught since she insisted on swinging right. The King arrived with his entourage and guests, and a crowd of the populace were herded by Swadis behind a rope fence. An agitated Sgt. Chapman espied the intruder of the morning very close to the King, and his anxious enquiry of the Service Police elicited that the morning's intruder was a Royal bodyguard, merely surveying the geography of the airport. Sgt. Chapman retired to his control tower.

The ensuing display with our clapped-out aeroplane impressed the spectators. We gave the boy king a ride in our DH 86 from which he surveyed his capital on the Tigris. Before leaving for Habbaniya in the Oxford, with Harry as an unwilling passenger, we beat up the aerodrome at nought feet plus, making the crowds duck as we shot between the hangars and up into a climbing turn. Props raised the dust, and the Oxford climbed away at 180 miles per hour. A reprimand awaited me in the bosses' office, for an unofficial display, but it was tempered by a congratulatory phone call from Air Vice Marshall Champion de Crespigny from Air Headquarters, Paiforce (wherever that was – Baghdad I think).

Now Royal Air Force, Habbaniya, as well as having

stables where hacks could be hired and officers' horses housed, also had a racetrack. In April a race meeting was organised by Group Captain Attwood, to which civilian horses were invited, as were the entire bookmaking fraternity of Baghdad. No race appeared to be more than four furlongs, but I don't recall winning in any race at all. Came the Station Stable race and mounted officers lined up at the start. They're off! But no! One well-groomed little horse ridden by Squadron Leader Beamish, the dentist, was well left. The race was re-run after the judges had decided that Sqn. Ldr. Beamish had been impeded at the start. This time the Squadron Leader got a flying start, winning easily since the other horses were knackered from their first attempt! I lost my money. Then followed a race which included all the camp hacks, a motley dispirited lot. Bets were placed and the horses lined up for the start, when suddenly the tannoy announced two late entries. Two gloriously groomed, magnificent stallions appeared, ridden by two Armenians of the Assyrian Levies. What a fiddle! The new entrants came in first and second by a mile, carrying only the money of those in the know. I know who they were, but must not name them.

Not long after this race meet, the warrant officer i/c the RAF police was posted to the UK, time expired. Rumour had it that he had extended his tour but was finally diagnosed and sent home. However he only got as far as Cairo before he was returned to Habbaniya, to face trial with other officers including the group captain, for, amongst many other things, selling MT spares and tyres to the civilian black market. Slightly used lorry tyres fetched two hundred Iraqi dinars, since they were otherwise unobtainable. Certain airmen, returning from leave, found that it was worthwhile bringing back a one-dinar bicycle tyre. It would sell for twenty times as much. As a result of the courts martial that followed at least six officers were found guilty and sentenced. The group captain was the only officer that I knew of to be cashiered in war-time. The warrant officer policeman served a long sentence as an airman, in his own field punishment centre. I imagine that many of his former subordinates revelled in the reversal.

Of all the flying in Iraq, I enjoyed the early morning meteorological climb most. It meant a slightly earlier than usual rise but flying the Gladiator in the cool of the early morning was exhilarating. Besides, any hangover soon dispersed with a few whiffs of oxygen. In fact the Gladiator cockpit was better than a bottle of aspirins. We generally climbed to 22,000 feet, reading the temperatures at every 500 feet as we went and making notes on the visibility. The thermometer was strapped to a strut on the wing and was generally reckoned to be more accurate than the one in the cockpit. It was quite an art and one never fully mastered, but the mixture had to be manually weakened as the aircraft climbed, and whenever I tried to reach the aircraft's ceiling, the engine would cut out, and not regain power till some height had been wound off. On return to earth the reading would be presented to the meteorological officer in his hut.

On my second climb, on 23rd April 1943, the Gladiator conveyed me to 29,770 feet. The Met. Officer sounded disbelieving. Then, some twenty met. climbs later, and after much practice with the mixture lever, I set off, on 10th July in a thick sand haze. The ground disappeared at a few hundred feet, and the Glad. sped into the clear at around 1200 feet. Nothing could be seen but a blue sky, and I climbed on a westerly heading. All went well and after 20,000 feet I circled, gaining height. At 29,000 feet the Glad. hung on its nose. The ASI read less than 100 mph. Still it inched higher and finally at 33,000 feet, wallowing crazily and hanging on its prop, the ceiling was reached. With throttle closed we lost height in an easterly direction. The Glad. had no radio. It was a very lonely feeling. A sand haze blotted out the ground, up to a height of 1000 feet. From that height we cautiously descended. My plan was to keep the eyes peeled and fly eastwards until the Euphrates was identified. What then? North or south? I made up my mind to fly north, having reasoned that the wind had been north of west against me in the climb. The flat ground came into view in the murk and I flew slowly east. After flying for a long time over unrecognisable territory, the river came up running north to south, just ahead. The Lord was thanked. A bank to port and the winding, wide muddy river was followed northwards towards Falluja and Habbaniya. On and on I flew, peering anxiously ahead in the dust-laden air. Then suddenly I was flying over a city. Baghdad? Obviously the wrong river. I had followed the Tigris! Left turn. Followed the road back to Habbaniya, a further sixty miles. I landed, still in the haze, with sticky hands, and underpants, cellular, airmen for the use of. I handed my weather climb records quite nonchalantly to the Met. Officer, who stared at them quite disbelievingly. I told Bumfrey that my delay was solely due to the dust haze. Later that morning I was to receive apologies from the met. man, who found the readings to be too accurate to be figments of my imagination. The height of 33,000 feet was 8000 feet higher than I was to reach again until 1971 in a jet aircraft. Some kite that Gladiator!

Towing drogues with the Audax whilst the Indian Army opened fire with Bren guns strapped to Bofors barrels was just as hair-raising, since I saw no published manual on the practice. By trial and error I learned to pass well out of range before making a reverse run. The reason? Well I often found that the drogue was between me and the Indian gunners, so I was in the firing line! A mock dog fight between Flight Sergeant Barfoot in an Audax and Sgt. Stacey (RCAF) in a Gladiator convinced me that the latter was far superior. The Audax stalled out of tight turns before the Glad., and I broke off the engagement, checking that I had brought my parachute.

The day of the swimming sports found me on the mail run to Baghdad. On the return I headed the Valentia into wind at 200 feet above the swimming pool, and throttled back to forty two miles per hour. With a headwind of forty miles per hour we had a grandstand view, and hovered effortlessly, if noisily above. A stronger gust of wind and we would have gone into reverse. Had the wind suddenly dropped we'd have joined the swimmers.

Then there was the Vickers Wellesley; very nerve-racking. A huge geodetic single-engined monoplane, with two enclosed cockpits and a huge flexing pair of wings; confidence was drained rather than bolstered. It seemed under-powered, but it had flown non-stop from Cairo to Darwin. It needed to be pushed around the sky, the control cables seemed made of elastic, and it had the uncanny knack of dropping its tail onto the runway first, when landing. Soda Whisky was to fly a wing commander to Cairo in our Wellesley, when an erring erk accidentally pulled up the undercarriage and bent the prop. Soda had the aircraft lifted and the prop removed. He supervised the straightening of the prop between two large planks, using a motor roller and, a day late, Soda and the Wingco made Cairo. How did she fly? 'Jost a leetle more shaking,' said Soda!

11th September 1943 approached. It was my twenty-first birthday and preparations were afoot to make it a memorable day. I recall that I bought twenty-one bottles of whisky at seven shillings and sixpence a bottle, and tinned New Zealand butter was available. The camp baker baked rolls and a birthday cake. The camp butcher supplied a huge roast of beef, and the mess provided all the Black Label Canadian beer that we might need. The whole mess, including the ape, joined the party and the day was mine after the met. climb in the morning, which I undertook with all fingers crossed. Birthdays had been my undoing. It was a wonderful night, but one which I would gladly have given up for an hour or two at home.

On 28th September 1943, with Plt. Off. Kerr as co-pilot, and carrying a wireless op we set out for Baghdad where we picked up a dozen stretcher cases, all with TB, and a few nurses. Airborne again we made for H 3, an airstrip on the pipeline to Haifa. The air was very turbulent and soon all patients, nurses, wireless op and Plt. Off. Kerr were sick. The smell coming up from the rear was overpowering – all smells come forward in a non-pressurised aircraft. I had to open the cabin door to the patients to give them air, but had to kneel on my seat with my head in the slipstream to prevent myself from retching. H 3 came up. We landed safely, refuelled, gave the nurses and crew time to recover, then were airborne again, making for Lydda airport in Palestine. Twenty miles from Lydda we came up with a Walrus, and a few extra revs meant that we in a Val had found an aircraft which we could out-distance. One up for the RAF – the other bod was a navy type. Stretcher types were bound for hospital in Haifa before a trip Blighty-side. The trip back to Habbaniya via H 3 was without incident. I note then that ten days later I took two VIPs to Baghdad in the Wellesley. I must have been petrified – wonder if the VIPs knew?

A special trip to Shaibah, to accompany the delivery of Hurricanes and Spitfires to the Russian pilots at Abadan, meant another meeting with Sqn. Ldr. Rev. P. Johnston. As the fighters were delivered I was to collect the pilots and fly them back to Shaibah to pick up some more fighters, landed by sea at Basra and built at the maintenance unit at Shaibah. I had promised Peter Johnston a ride, but before that could take place, I broke the Oxford. I joined the circuit at Abadan with the Hurricanes and landed short, behind them. Too short – I struck a sand wall with such force, just as I was levelling out, that only a huge heave on the stick prevented a messy business. This wall was fifty yards before the runway, had sloping sides and cast no shadow. The Oxford lurched back into the air, throttles opened wide, whilst one wheel lay below, on the wall. Consternation – what to do? The advice on the control panel was no help. 'If you must prang, prang at an M.U.' Now the nearest maintenance unit was Shaibah but I was not thinking straight. Circling Abadan with just one wheel hanging loosely down, I noticed the hospital complex on the north side of the airfield. A group of tents. It was a beautiful belly landing, skidding across the sand, to end up fifty yards from the fire engine and fifteen yards from the hospital entrance. I needed no attention, but the aircraft did.

The next few days were spent in hospital back at Habbaniya with a severe attack of sandfly fever. Temperature 105 degrees, I was put on 'M and B', a sulphonamide I think. Felt very ropey, but was about in five days, when I received another surprise. A medical orderly praised my beautiful little body, and scared me out of that hospital in quick time. My first brush with a homosexual.

Back on duty we learned that Air Vice Marshall Champion de Crespigny was getting a bit anxious about the dwindling number of aircraft under his command, and we were all lined up alongside the taxying track to await his arrival from Baghdad in his personal Hart. I must say that I was very anxious, and felt that his visit had been caused by my recent prang. His Hawker Hart was in the circuit. 'Properly at ease. Atten-shun.' A dozen or so pilots stood to attention in newly starched KD. The Hart approached, did a wheely, then, whoops, up on its nose! Poetic justice? I dunno, but we avoided the lecture as a dishevelled Air Vice Marshall arranged his immediate flight back to Baghdad in the DH 86! My logbook was endorsed in red at the back. 'Gross carelessness – undershooting, when landing Oxford aircraft

L.4668 at RAF Station Abadan, on 9th. April, 1943, 1268865 Flt. Sgt. Barfoot struck a four foot high bank, causing damage to the aircraft.' An understatement!

During that summer of 1943 I recall an American aircraft landing at Habbaniya in the early evening. Jack Benny and his concert party climbed out, and the camp theatre was packed that night as Jack Benny introduced the show.

'We were on our way to the American Forces in the Persian Gulf when we received word that an aircraft flying south after dusk might be shot down. We knew our show was bad, but not that bad. So we were persuaded to night stop and give you a show.'

The singer was an auburn-haired Peggy Lee, who invited an airman on the stage to assist her. She sang to him and ruffled his hair. It took her ages to release herself from his enveloping arms as he entered into the spirit of the thing, urged on by a thousand love-starved airmen! How lucky can you get! The following morning I descended from my met. climb to fly in formation with the departing concert party.

Later that year Lord Louis Mountbatten arrived to night stop, on his way to India to take up his command of the Far Eastern Theatre, Lord Louis disembarked, followed by at least a dozen beautiful Wren officers. Ladies in waiting? He was envied by the whole camp. Twenty-one years later he was to spot my Burma Star as he embarked in his Comet in Labuan, North Borneo. From the top of the aircraft steps he turned, marched down the steps again and questioned me about my Far Eastern service. I forgave him his entourage of 1943. He had the common touch.

And so the summer passed. At 125 degrees Fahrenheit in the shade we were glad it was not humid. I joined the camp rovers and we ran ten troops of boy scouts amongst the children of the Assyrian Levies. Ben Eshoo was my troop leader and they were grand kids. I was entrusted with a pass to the civilian cantonment, where we once put on a variety show. We marched them to Lake Habbaniya on occasion, where we swam amongst mica outcrops. Short Sunderlands landed on the lake on their way to and from India. The cook at the transit camp near the lake often found the temperature in his corrugated iron cook-house to be 160 degrees Fahrenheit! He rushed in and out swathed in wet blankets. I treasure a letter from Ben Eshoo who wrote, 'Dear Fly Sergeant, I hope you are not yet dead. When we meet bring me a watch.' Where are those Armenians and Assyrians now? Eventually the nurses at the camp hospital ran three troops of girl guides, some in purdah. I treasure, too, the numerous photographs, including some when we were inspected by the nobs from scouting headquarters in London. I wonder, did the Germans run scout troops?

Now, on 4th July 1942, my sister's birthday, I had pranged *H for Harry* at Abu Suier. On 5th July 1942, I pranged *B for Bertie*; it was my father's birthday. On 18th October 1943, my fiancée's birthday, I was due to make morning met. climb, and I was very, very careful. I wasn't careful enough. A tyre burst on landing, the Gladiator 6147 swerved across the bundoo and the two starboard wings made contact with the ground. They folded up and I looked rather like a Swordfish of the Fleet Air Arm, with only one side folded. Whether it was repaired I don't know. If not, it left but one to continue with the met. climbs. I was always chary of flying on people's birthdays thereafter but, at the risk of losing my nickname of 'Pranger', I will emphasise now that I never, never broke another aeroplane. More by luck than judgement. That's not quite true – I did severely damage a Fortress, and I wasn't even in it.

On 24th October W/O Bessen and I set off with Bombay 5812, a recent acquisition, for Shaibah, Bahrain and Sharjah. It was at Sharjah that we took aboard an engine for a long-nosed Blenheim of 224 Squadron, operating from Masirah

Island, which had forced-landed at Shinas, a sheikdom on the eastern side of the Sharjah peninsula. Shinas turned out to be a landing ground outside an Arab village with an ancient fort. We landed to deposit a ground crew with tools and equipment to make the required engine change. W/O Bessen, the wireless operator and I were invited to meet the sheik who lived in this tumbledown fort, and on passing through his village, where the tiny passageways were roofed over, we were led to a tunnel which passed as the entrance to the fort. Inside the tunnel were a few guards with ancient long-barrelled rifles, guarding a bound man who looked terrified. We were led into a huge room, at one end of which was a huge king-sized bed, a semicircle of at least 10 feet radius, covered with cushions and rich silks. At the other end sat the sheik with an interpreter, and various pleasantries followed before a bowl of millet or sago was put before us. It looked terrible, but we quickly realised it was a sacrifice, and endeavoured to eat it. Now it is most difficult to pick up sago cooked in goats' milk with one's fingers, and the interpreter, realising our difficulty, sent for a spoon, which we all had to share. Ugh! The sheik asked us if we would like to attend his court. He would be trying a thief for stealing. The bound man? The interpreter conveyed the sheik's invitation, adding 'Don't! If he is guilty they will cut off his right hand in the court.' We offered the sheik a ride in the Bombay at a later date, and declined his generous offer.

On the way back through the smelly market I bought two lengths of cloth. One was silk which, made into a light dressing gown, I still wear in the summer. Back at the plane we met the sheik's son and his bodyguard, and showed the young lad the cockpit. Outside our airmen were trying to persuade one of the bodyguard to discharge his huge rifle. The bullets were cast in lead and the huge half-inch cartridges were hand-charged, and hand-polished in beautiful brass. We discovered that they could not fire their rifles without the prince's permission. He gave it. A guard depressed the loading platform on his huge long-barrelled rifle, and slid a shell into the breech. Apprehensively he aimed at a barrel, pulled the trigger and nothing happened. He loaded a second time, with the same result. With the third home-made shell he was less lucky. There was a mighty explosion and a huge hole was put in the old oil barrel. The guard nursed an injured shoulder, and wiped a blackened but triumphant face. We returned to Sharjah where the evening was hot and one hundred per cent humid. Alcoholic drinks were banned by the Sultan of Sharjah so the evening was spent imbibing pints of fresh lime juice. The water was so salty that salt-water soap had to be used to wash or shower. Rumour had it that outside the gates of Sharjah were two huge brass muzzle-loading cannons to which miscreants were tied whilst they were flogged. The drinking of alcohol merited such treatment.

The night was humid, quiet but for a chirruping of crickets. The hut was full of nude and snoring men when suddenly there was a cry from across the room. 'Help, help! Get off my chest,' and an airman opposite leaped out of bed, ran down the hut, tried to dash through the doorway into the night, but stubbed his toe on the protruding threshold. Amazed I watched him stagger back to bed. On the very next night he gave a repeat performance. He got his boat ticket!

On the following day it was off to Shinas, where we landed early. A message for us stated that the sheik would not be flying in an aeroplane with one wing. It appeared that, some years before, a Wapiti biplane had forced-landed nearby. The sheik had been offered thousands of rupees to have a road built to the landing ground so that the plane could be pulled to it. His villagers had done this, and the sheik had eventually been given a ride in the Wapiti. Later he was paid but a fraction of what he had been promised and quite understandably he did not trust the British again.

A queue awaited us by the airmen's tent. A sick parade – the sick of the village turned up for aspirin and codeine. However, one Arab couple had brought their young baby for treatment. The unwinding of saturated rags displayed a recently circumcised little winkle in a very sore state. Iodine was diluted with good clean drinking water from the aircraft water bottles and the wound was cleansed. What then? It was too small for a bandage. Ointment, probably vaseline, was liberally applied, a field dressing was fixed in place with sticking plaster, and a grateful Mum and Dad took a quieter little patient away. I hope he survived.

We left Shinas to go to Masirah, via Ras el Had, to pick up tools and spares. At Ras el Had we saw that a Blenheim had gone off the end of the runway, and was practically immersed in the sea. We were interested to watch the salvage operation. A large dhow had been anchored alongside the submerged aircraft. A rope was secured to a cradle round the fuselage, and was passed through a huge pulley affixed to the dhow's mast. Dozens of Arabs were lined up grasping the rope and, to a chant, they started to haul on the rope and rapidly made their way across the bundoo. Unfortunately the aircraft didn't move at all. At each step the mast of the dhow got nearer and nearer to the horizontal. A frantic dhow skipper just got through to the mob in time.

Masirah island was the home for 224 Coastal Command Squadron, whose job it was to patrol the Gulf against German or Japanese submarines. Rumours far exceeded sightings. The island had no fresh water of its own. Daily water was brought over in dhows from the mainland. It is rumoured that Captain Kidd's treasure was buried thereon and both prewar and afterwards, the island has been thoroughly searched. I think Malcolm Campbell once had hopes. It did however have an open-air cinema where a film was shown until the next one arrived.

Spares loaded, it was back to Shinas. The Blenheim was soon airworthy and, once it had flown out, we departed for Habbaniya and a bath, some nine hundred miles north. At Bahrain we picked up some Indian men, women and children, about twenty all told. Where they had come from and where they were eventually going I did not know. As we approached Kuwait an engine cut out. Now a Bombay can barely fly on two engines in such heat, so on one we were lucky to make the Kuwait airfield – which was just a flat expanse. No one saw us land. The town of Kuwait was miles away. Then the wireless operator had a bright idea. We dragged out the trailing aerial and the operator was able to raise Shaibah, who by telephone instructed the British Consul in Kuwait that we were on his airfield! Certainly within half an hour the consul arrived by car at the airfield together with the only two taxis in the place. I cannot remember how we and our passengers were transported by the cars, nor how we secured the aircraft. I do remember that I, together with the Indian families, was taken to a house in Kuwait which was single-storeyed and built round a courtyard. It was a house reserved for such emergencies, and was fully equipped with kitchen, beds, linen, other furniture and some tinned food. Every room opened out into the same central courtyard and here we were, isolated and hoping that the stay would be extended. The political agent advised that I keep a taxi on call, and told me to charge any purchases of food or necessities to his account. The local market was colourful, and supplied all our needs. Two days later on 6th November, a Valentia arrived with spares and groundcrew, and departed for Baghdad with our civilian passengers. By 7th November, Bristol Bombay 5812 was serviceable enough to drag us to Shaibah, so we said farewell to the American doctor, his wife, and the political agent. As I remember it, there were but three buildings in Kuwait at that time. After night-stopping at Shaibah we arrived at Habbaniya on 8th November. I was questioned about a bill for 800 rupees which had been received from that political agent, on an imprest.

I was to find that I was again posted. To Blighty? Not on your Nelly! With 922 hours under my belt I was posted to Transport Command in Cairo, at their disposal. There was a helluva party and my farewells were said to Communications Flight personnel and to Soda Whisky. My scouts were sorry to wave farewell as I left westwards on the Nairn cross-desert bus. Bus and trailer were full of service personnel and one Polish woman from the Polish camp outside Baghdad. She was in British WRAC uniform. Hundreds of Polish people, mostly women, had been released from prison and work camps in Siberia and had been transferred, via Teheran, to convalescent camps near Baghdad.

It was with very mixed feelings that I watched the flesh-pots of Habbaniya recede into the distance. Harry Dawson was to see out his tour at Habbaniya, even to become a traitor and accept a commission. After all he had only broken one aircraft at Habbaniya – their only, and his second, Hudson! Bob Mann, still on No. 4 METS and on hard times as a commissioned pilot flying a Dakota at Rosh Pinnar in Palestine, had also turned traitor. I was the only one of the three musketeers still in the lower echelon.

The pumping station H 3 came up and went, then we stopped for a break in the desert. The men on board relieved themselves at the rear of the bus, but the poor Polish girl set out to walk over the flat horizon into the distance to ease the pressure. She had only to ask, and we would all have gone to one side of the bus. As it was she spent our twenty-minute stop just walking into the distant distance.

I probably arrived in Cairo about 15th November 1943,

and spent a few days at the aircrew mess of Number 1 Aircraft Delivery Unit in Heliopolis. Air Commodore Witney-Straight had some connection therewith. This unit seemed to be full of Aussies and Poles. Their task was to be flown to Takoradi on the Gold Coast, there to pick up and ferry aircraft back, mostly Spitfires and Hurricanes I believe.

All day long these pilots, well most of them, gambled at brag or poker or crap. The stakes, up to fifty Egyptian pounds, were phenomenal, at least ten weeks pay! I kept a low profile. Then rumour had it that these pilots were involved in smuggling. The norm was to take a case of watches from Cairo to Takoradi. There the watches were exchanged for snakeskins which represented a fiftyfold increase in capital gain per trip. Those playing for high stakes dealt in gold from the west coast. Rumour had it that many a pilot-type parachute hid the watches and the snakeskins. The parachute was removed! All pilots were being scrutinised by the Service Investigation Unit who knew the game. Large accounts were amassed in Cairo banks. Greek and French businessmen offered large dowries to those who would marry their daughters. One Polish pilot under suspicion avoided apprehension. He was supposed to deal in gold. He did not return from one trip and his crashed Hurricane was not found for months, until it was spotted near Wadi Natrun by a ferry pilot. The aircraft and his skeleton were salvaged, and the 20mm gun barrels were found to be the hiding places for the gold!

On 26th November I joined a Dakota flight at LG 224, Cairo West, to be flown by Plt. Off. Weir of 216 Squadron to Oujda in Morocco, via Benina, Castel Benito and Biskra, where we stayed in a luxury hotel, the Atlantique. It was a beautiful place in the middle of the Sahara, owned by the French Shipping Line. A very magnetic place.

At Oujda I found myself on a former French airfield, and

posted to Number 3 Aircraft Delivery Unit. Here I had time to ponder and recall those pre-war days and the circumstances which had led to Flight Sergeant Barfoot's arrival at yet another unit in yet another theatre. If you will forgive me, this might be the point where such detail can be recorded. I will understand if you wish to by-pass the next chapter and pick up when current action starts again.

SCHOOLDAYS, THE OUTBREAK OF WAR AND DAD'S ARMY

August 1939 brought the School Certificate results; A1 they were for East Sussex and excellent for the son of a World War I private in the Royal Engineers. What next? University was not a natural progression for a working man's son in 1939, hence a compromise – Higher Schools Certificate in mathematics and physics with a part time Inter. BSc (Engineering) course at Brighton Technical College.

Earlier in that year the local territorial army company, containing many young men a year or so older than I, was called to the colours and shipped off to camp. Parents waved goodbye at the railway station, all mindful of the Great War. Hearts were heavy, though hope remained. 'Terriers' themselves went as if to summer camp, with a sense of independence, some apprehension, and a very real optimism that somehow war could be avoided. 'Peace in our time' had been promised. That promise could not be kept.

Schooldays from 1934, when I gained a scholarship to Lewes County Secondary School, until I left on 17th June 1940, had been satisfying, though not altogether uneventful. A second broken leg at rugby in 1936 led to a disappointing tenth place in the annual cross country of 1937. In every other year second had been my lowest place. In 1938 I captained the school 2nd XV and a year later was a member of the 1st XV. During 1938 and 1939 I rehearsed my medium-paced bowling and cross-batted swings with the first XI. What spare time there was after cricket, rugger, school and homework, I spent as a patrol leader of the Bulldogs in the sixth Seaford St Leonard's troop, as a regular member of the Bible class, and Bible class club. This club was opened at the Simmons Institute every Saturday night, and the twelve of us played table tennis, billiards and darts. Of the twelve, I believe all went into the Royal Air Force, at least eight as pilots and six of those pilots returned.

A bosom friend of mine, Eddie, who had been so for six years by then, was one who didn't come back. Relegated to flying gliders on the Rhine crossing in 1945, he did not live to reach the ground. Marande, an old Lewesian and another pilot with whom Eddie had trained, saw it all happen. Eddie was one of fifty-seven Old Lewesians whose promising life was extinguished. I would hazard that more than half of the fifty-seven were aircrew. Eddie developed an avid and knowledgeable interest in birds of the feathered variety and the interest he encouraged in me often meant that we were to be found in mid-winter at Cuckmere Haven, lying flat on our bellies in the snow stalking a red-throated diver or a kingfisher.

Lest it be thought that existence was monastic, I must admit to a short infatuation with the stationmaster's daughter (many an 0837 had set off for Lewes as late as 0840, if Joan and I were late). However Kitty, my sister's school friend, eventually emerged from her shyness to deign to walk with 'that boy Barfoot', some six months or so before war broke out. A sort of destiny perhaps, since my mother and Kitty's had been school friends in their day. Life was full, and never boring. There was never ever 'nothing to do'; sport, the South Downs, the seaside, school and homework filled the week, every week. How I found time to make Kitty aware of my interest from the age of 16 onwards I don't know but, by the summer of 1940, that interest had the biggest priority. On 11th September 1939, with the war declared and at the age of 17, Kitty and I stood that fine evening outside Edward's store in Steyne Road, and wondered where we might find ourselves at the age of 21. I well remembered this incident, especially when in 1943 I happened to be 60 miles from Baghdad on my 21st birthday, having left England some two years before.

Hitler, having bluffed and challenged an ill-prepared Europe over Czechoslovakia and Austria, marched on to Poland. I remember little about that. War talk was in the air, and I heard Neville Chamberlain announce that, no answer having been received from Herr Hitler to our ultimatum, Great Britain and the British Empire now considered themselves at war with Germany. On the day I learned this, I was at my father's garage where I spent two hours serving petrol – it was 3rd September 1939. At about 11 o'clock on that morning, a bright, breezy one, I set off to walk to my home, but had only proceeded about 100 yards when the newly installed siren in Sutton Drove wailed earnestly. The sky looked bright and peaceful, clouds scudded, the fluctuating siren put a very heavy and ominous feeling in the heart, and eyes automatically scanned the sky – nothing to see. My pace quickened to reach 'St. Anselms', our home in Stafford Road. The house seemed deserted. It was built on a steep hill so that the entrance at road level was into the middle one of three floors. My small and somewhat damp bedroom was on the lower floor and was sheltered at the front of the house by a steep bank. I descended to it and stopped, puzzled and amazed to find my sister Mary and our mutual friend Kitty feverishly dipping newspapers into flour paste and endeavouring to fill the ventilator and cracks in the windows. Whilst tears streamed down their faces, they were endeavouring to make my bedroom gas-proof before the Hun arrived, as promised by the sirens. My laughter was a bit forced, I must admit. I

120

The aged Dak crew more than 35 years on. Nicky Nicholas, Dick Sheppard, George Telford, the author.

Vickers Wellington Ic by Edwin Knowles who lost his life on the Rhine crossing, flying a glider.

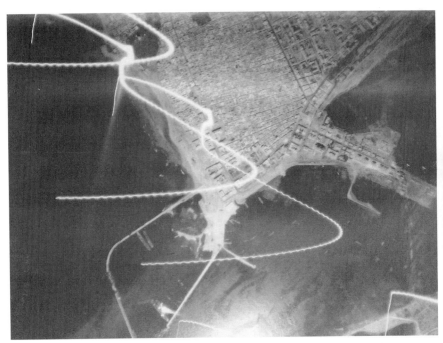

Bombing Benghasi from 13,000 ft on 6th April 1942. Airspeed 110 mph; course 120 degrees. Skipper Wg. Cdr. J.H.T. Simpson DSO, DFC. Co-pilot the author. Navigator Fg. Off. Nick Mansell. W/Op. Sgt. O.G. Ackerman. Gunners: Sgts. D. Acland and Mick Navin.

Free from infection: The artist was Dick Field, a ground radar operator.

Valentias: Dropping Assyrian Levies at Habbaniya.

A Dakota: Dusk at Bari: 6th October 1944.

A truck load: Hardworking ground crew at Bari.

Loading Casualties: Greece, December 1944.

hugged them both, as reassuringly as a school boy could, but now I realise that, had their fears been substantiated, we three might have been the only survivors in Seaford!

Later in the war we collected our gas masks and ration books, put up our black-outs, accepted our evacuees, and filled the ranks of the local defence volunteers, 'Dad's Army', later to be the Home Guard. The Home Guard who, according to a later famous leader, would spill blood in the sea, on the beaches, in the countryside and in the towns, should Jerry try to walk in. The winter of 1939–40, with no street lamps and a liberal amount of freezing rain and black ice, was extremely perilous. Then I realised that my night vision was faulty and I often suffered the pleasant indignity of being led by Kitty when I took her home. How I returned on my own I don't remember.

Where, how and under what persuasion I joined the ranks of the local Defence Volunteers I don't know. I have a vague recollection of 'being fell in' in Broad Street, having been allocated to a company about 12 strong led by Lord Buckmaster, a tall World War I veteran; I believe the poor old fellow was just recovering from a painful divorce. At 17 years old I found myself in the company of 11 old soldiers, only some of whom I had previously known. How we came to be allocated a guard post at Edward's Barn on Seaford Head just north of Hope Gap and west of Cuckmere Haven, I don't know either. There the company were on guard duty from 8 pm until 6 am, two nights per week. Deterrence was based initially on two shot guns, a pistol, two old bayonets and Lord Buckmaster's sabre, together with a few robust scout staves and a sheath knife or two. At the barn we did our 'two on and four off' until daybreak, watching for the expected invasion. The 'two on' were spent in lonely isolation and trepidation in our observation post on top of a straw stack 30 yards south of the barn, whilst the first 'four off', at least, were spent playing nap for halfpennies. I was

121

taught the game by Messrs Taylor, Gray and Hopkins so well that I invariably went off duty at least a whole shilling richer than when I arrived. 'Players' were 11½d for 20, 'Woodbines' were 8d, beer was 4d a pint and the front row of the balcony at the Ritz was 9d, so I realise I gave insufficient sympathy to the misfortunes of Mr Gray, Bravery's pantechnicon driver, who invariably supplied the major part of my winnings. His pay at the time would not have exceeded 50 shillings a week, and he had a big family.

With the phoney war on, and Dunkirk and the fall of France not far ahead, we were issued with Ross .30 Canadian Rifles of WWI vintage. Each was presented with pull through, oil bottle, four by two, smarmed in grease and flecked with straw. How eagerly it was cleaned and polished! The barrel, all of twenty-five years old, gleamed between the pit marks. An absence of a rifle sling meant some very individualistic cord work between the upper and lower swivels. An old soldier was very serious when he intoned that it had a range of three miles, but that, since we were rationed to five rounds each, it might be advisable to let the enemy get a bit closer. One bullet, he said, would penetrate the bodies of twenty-one Germans if they were to attack in close line astern.

During that spring, 1940, I attended the ladies' toilets opposite the Salts (swept away by the storms of 1947), which had been surrounded by sandbags and was an observation post over the Seaford bay. Here an officer appeared to give me some training 'on the range', to see if I knew which way to point the gun. The sea was rough and the wind gusty and full of rain. Through the grey and salt-laden air I finally made out a float, some 150 yards from the shore, rising and falling with the waves. Three rounds were loaded into the magazine, I was ordered to point the rifle in the general direction of the target, to put a round up the spout, to aim and squeeze, not pull, the trigger. There was an almighty explosion and I felt a thump in the shoulder.

'Pull the butt into your shoulder, aim and squeeze.' The next bang was just as fearsome and the bruise was aggravated. The examiner said, 'Fair shot.' I saw nothing and suspect that neither did he.

'Fire the third round.' After an interminable time I thought the target rose into view – a snatch at the trigger, a deafening explosion and a sharp pain.

'Never saw it,' said the officer. That made two of us. I returned home having passed my marksmanship test, to put some embrocation on my shoulder, and to clean the rifle.

With petrol severely rationed my father did not demur when I left school on 17th June 1940; business had collapsed and I thought I could and should earn my keep. With the help of Neville R. Bradshaw MA (Oxon), my headmaster, I obtained a job in a test laboratory at Allen West, on the Lewes Road in Brighton. Here I endeavoured to test starters and controllers for electric motors. I recall there were three little pots full of transformer oil which somehow operated three solenoids when the green button was pushed. The trip and the reset button had to be tested. Power was tapped off from live, uninsulated cables which ran just overhead. Hooks on the end of wooden handles were placed over the wires, cables were connected to the hooks and crocodile clips were at the other end of the wires. One had to remember to disconnect the hooks before disconnecting the crocodile clips, but quite often one did not! The overhead lines were supposed to carry 600 volts. I can well believe it. I sampled all of them almost daily and developed a palsy-like tremble of the hands.

A week's work consisted of sixty hours, which included one spell of overtime from 6 pm to 10 pm spent in 'control' of thirty resistance winders, all female. With some kind of bridge, resistors were checked within specified limits. Orders to rewind were often met with an unprintable response. Almost invariably the air raid sounded at some time during the shift and much of it was spent in the air-raid shelter. An innocent seventeen-year-old was frequently incarcerated in the dark with thirty resistance winders. Education did not only take place in schools!

The first week was pay-less – we were paid for one week after two weeks work, to facilitate the administration. I suspect it was really to keep a vast sum away from the workers as long as possible. At the end of the second week I lined up for my hard earned wages. The envelope said '48 hours at 2½d and 12 hours at 3.125d/hour', not quite 13/- with stoppages. I refused the envelope and denied that I had consented to such a pittance. I had a word with Bob Wynter, an old Lewesian and contemporary who seemed to be doing well in the drawing office. He denied any influence, though he was walking out with a director's daughter. Called before an executive some two days later I was informed that the manager of the test department got £3-0-0. per week, however many hours he did, and the chief tester had to be satisfied with £2-4-6 as a basic wage. How much did I think I was worth? 'Fivepence an hour,' I said, and, for my cheek, that was what I was promised from then on. The wage packet usually said £1-5-5 each week. Nine shillings for Mother, nine shillings for busfares and a whole seven shillings and fivepence to squander on clothes, lunches, leisure and brilliantine.

By some juggling and borrowing I was soon able to buy a Coventry Eagle 150 cc 2-stroke for £3. I travelled to work in style and became the Home Guard despatch rider. By some sharp practice I acquired a licence to drive ambulances. I never drove one but the police seemed to think it would cover a motorcycle as well. It wasn't long before I was forced into a sliding dismount on racecourse hill, as a double-decker bus turned right in front of me. The bike went under the bus. I watched on my backside in the middle of the road, as both chromium-plated flexible exhausts were fractured. My arrival at Edwards farm that night was announced by a throaty roar and orange flames.

On guard from 10 pm until midnight outside the barn I was rudely awakened by the guard commander, Lord Buckmaster, sword in hand. He was entitled to be rude as he gravely explained how sleeping guards could be court-martialled and shot. Besides they let the company down. Marvellous man; I still wonder whether he told the rest of the company. On guard again from 4 am until 6 am, this time perched on top of a haystack, in bright moonlight and awaiting the dawn, I was wide awake and watchful. Click, click, click. Someone had cocked a rifle, and quite nearby too. I hit the base of the stack expeditiously, realising what a silhouette I presented on the stack. Courageously I yelled 'Call out the guard', and heard Lord Buckmaster and my comrades curse as they stumbled across the barn-yard.

'What have you seen, Barfoot?' asked the Lord, presenting his sabre.

'Nothing,' said I, 'but I heard someone cock a rifle.'

Lord Buckmaster bravely prodded the stack and some nearby bushes, the company following him. Nothing was found; they all departed. Later, all quiet and sitting at the base of the stack, click, click, click, click. It was dawn and the sounds came from a nearby rabbit warren where rabbits had started to gambol. They must have knocked stones together. This time I told no one.

Our guard post was changed to a tent at Cradle Valley, and my duty clashed with my late shift at Allen West's. Riding past the cemetery one night at 11 pm, along a narrow path with a masked headlamp, I became aware of some movement ahead in the inky darkness. With admirable speed I was off the bike on my belly, rifle pointing ahead.

Had the Hun arrived? Should I challenge and then fire? How did one surrender in safety? My fears were just as real as I backed into the bushes to let the cow go by! There was more excitement to come that night. Patrolling the track alone at the top of Cradle Valley, a rattling, squealing, clattering noise like a hundred armoured crusaders assailed my cold ears. There it was, an enemy tank for sure, coming straight at me. 'Halt! Who goes there?' I yelled before plunging into the gorse bushes to evade a seemingly blind Bren-gun carrier driver. Whether he was aware of me or not I'll never know. He roared off down the hill and up the valley towards Firle Beacon.

It was July 1940. Churchill was preparing us to 'fight on the beaches'. Invasion was in the air. Rumour was rife. Drums of petrol were sunk below the low water mark and placed at the crest of hill roads. If the Germans came someone would get burned. Kitty, her sister and her brother were evacuated to Leicester. I was playing tennis with Jean Godfrey, a sporting gal with an Eton crop. She was thrashing me. From the tennis court I saw the Heinkel 111 flying lazily in the sunshine between Newhaven and Seaford Head, at about 500 feet. He was probably photographing our defences, a six-inch naval gun in someone's garden and the ladies' lavatory surrounded with sandbags. Perhaps he was armed; perhaps he had bombs. I sprinted for the sheltered side of a thick four-foot high wall. The only time I beat Jean that day. There was a loud and familiar bang close by. A Home Guard had leapt from the aforementioned ladies' loo and had fired his Ross .30 at the Heinkel. Missed!

Then high above we saw him, a Spitfire. One Heinkel was near oblivion. We watched as a Spitfire dived. Nasty shock! The Spitfire became an ME 109 as it got nearer. Both enemy planes made off towards Beachy Head where, later rumour had it, they were intercepted and shot down. We didn't resume the tennis.

During August 1940 we were often forced to take shelter as waves of bombers crossed the south coast heading inland, mostly without escorts. On one occasion a Spitfire swept in amongst the rear formation, shot down a Heinkel and followed it down. The driver of the Spitfire did not look in his mirror. Another hefty Heinkel peeled off, tracked the Spit and shot it down before slowly climbing up to chase his formation. Not a single ack-ack gun fired. Later we learned that the Spit pilot was Polish, and later still we began to appreciate how much we owed to those Free Poles, whose courage was complemented by hate and a longing for revenge at any price. Man for man they accounted for twice as many enemy as anyone else. When all was over many fell on hard times, not daring then to go home.

On a Saturday at the end of August 1940, sea mist and low clouds rolled inland and obliterated Seaford from the eyes of the Luftwaffe. Around midday I heard an aircraft flying low, circling the town, and was convinced it was not friendly. The engine beat was unmistakable. The Huns seemed unable to synchronise their propellers. I fetched and loaded my Ross and stood peering skywards on the wooden stairs outside the back door of our flat over Bimbo's Garage. I don't know how long I waited, but I heard the plane coming lower and circling. Suddenly there it was. A Heinkel emerged from the mist, flying slowly. I bruised my shoulder again as I fired two rounds at it in quick succession. Confident that it would fall out of control, I could not believe it when it disappeared into the mist on an even keel. My disappointment soon turned to worry. How was I to explain my depleted stock of ammunition, now three rounds only? Then I remembered that my father had several as souvenirs from World War I, in his bedroom. At that time he was a Lüger armed volunteer coastguard.

When all was quiet, it must have been the very next day, I purloined three of those rounds from the desktop in Dad's

127

bedroom. I had to test one and hoped to make up the deficiency with the other two. In Sutton Corner Garage, 'Bimbo's', there was a long bench with a heavy vice. By mounting the rifle in the vice it could be directed at a cupboard on the back wall, some twenty-five feet away. On a shelf I placed three large wooden blocks, altogether some eighteen inches thick. A chalk cross on the wood was the aiming point. An almighty bang erupted when the rifle was fired and a blue haze lay between me and the target. With trepidation, lest I had missed, I approached the target and noticed with cocky satisfaction that it was a bull. I moved the first block – great splinters at the back. Moved the second block – bigger splinters at the back. Then the third block. A huge exit hole! Stooping and peering, I saw a great hole into daylight in the wall. The inside wall was breeze-block only and the outer was pebble-dashed brick. The hole was much bigger than .303 and let in a lot of daylight. Mr Moore's house was behind the wall – he had a German mother and ran the next-door riding stables. Apprehensively I went out, around the garage, down the stable yard and into his garden. The hole was not visible from the outside, as there was a row of rabbit hutches against the wall. An apprehensive search revealed a startled rabbit with a large hole above his head. The bullet must have hit the flint wall of Mr Moore's house, where I did not stay to see. By shifting the cupboard inside just a few inches the hole was covered. Whether it is still visible I don't know, but there must still be evidence in the south-east corner of the garage which at the time of writing is still a going concern. Rabbit must long since have died, taking my secret with him. It was thus confirmed to me that the old soldier was erring on the conservative side when he said that a point 303 would go through twenty-one Germans lined up astern. Point 303? Point 303? But it was only a point 30 Ross rifle! The marvel was that the barrel had not split. The .303 must

128

have left that barrel with the velocity of an anti-tank round. Had anyone heard the shot it would have been mistaken for a back-fire; a common occurrence in my father's garage. I often wonder if anyone ever fired those other two rounds from the shoulder, because they were eventually handed in with the rifle.

On 11th September the Hun came in force and lost a lot of aircraft. It was my eighteenth birthday and, at work, I was to receive a knock-out blow and four 250-volt electric shocks. As I stood at my test bench, trying to look as though I knew what I was doing, I was chatting with someone about the possible uses of certain controllers. Guesses had varied between tram cars and de-gaussing apparatus to counter magnetic mines. Vaguely I heard a tester on my left call out for a hammer. Then it happened. A blinding flash and oblivion. I believe that there was just time to think that that was the end of my war efforts. Coming round, slowly, I wondered which of the two well-advertised places I might find myself in, and was quite surprised to find myself horizontal alongside my bench. It appeared that some clot on my right had lobbed a hammer and shorted the bare 600-volt overhead cables with a flash, the hammer falling on my head. The four 250-volt shocks that followed were probably due to my befuddled state of mind and so, because war could not be more dangerous, I was soon at the RAF recruiting office near Brighton station begging to be enlisted as a pilot. A medic noticed my trembling fingers with disbelief. I was a bit young to be an alcoholic, but trembling out-stretched fingers did not augur well for the war effort. Much form filling, then home I went to wait.

On 15th September Jerry got his biggest bloody nose to date. Thank God for the Spitfires and Hurricanes and for those who flew them, they alone saved England. Claims were that 154 German aircraft were downed that day. The number was inflated, but the Battle of Britain in the air was

No. 3 AIRCRAFT DELIVERY UNIT

The reader – if reader there still is – may wonder at what stage the war was when I arrived in Morocco. During that wonderful interlude in Iraq, the British and Allied Forces had cleared north Africa without my help, and so a flight from Cairo along the north coast of Africa in a DC 3 of 216 Squadron was as near to my first scheduled airline flight as it could be.

I wondered what would be my fate. What aircraft were yet being delivered to the Middle East via Morocco? They certainly wouldn't be Valentias, Bombays, Gladiators or Wellesleys!

I was by now the proud wearer of one ribbon, the Africa Star, and was expecting the promulgation of my 'Tate and Lyle' at any time. It was overdue, unless my wrecking experiences had delayed it in any way.

Oujda was a former airfield of the French Colonial Air Force. There were permanent barracks in two storeys, with verandahs on one side. In November the weather was cool, so that the expeditions to those French free-standing, or stooping, water-closets were more a necessity than a relief. The unit did have three more erstwhile members of Communications Flight, Paiforce. Whether they were there on my arrival, or whether they turned up close behind me I can't remember. They were Sgt. Harvey, a nice quiet lad who used to go down to Fez to pick up Hurricanes and

Spitfires for onwards flight to Cairo, and Flight Sergeants Thibault (RCAF) and Campey (RAAF). What they flew, if indeed they did, I don't remember, but I do recall that the pair of them lived in a stone-built store, well away from the rest of us. They were very busy assembling a paraffin-burning central heating system while the rest of us froze. One day their patent furnace exploded and burned fiercely. It was their state of inebriation and the pervading smell which led to the discovery that the invention was really a still! They were thrown out of the local bistro when, in an inebriated sleep, one of them awoke to glimpse a female leg in close proximity to his chair. Surreptitiously the leg was stroked. The owner and her escort were outraged, and the Aussie fled with the French Canadian. Thibault was later to set a nest of matches in the welt of Campey's shoe. These he lit, giving Campey a hot foot. But they remained friends. Poor Sgt. Harvey met some atrocious weather over the mountains and was lost.

My flight commander was an Anglo-Indian, and having elicited that I flew Wellingtons he detailed a navigator, WO Gee, and a W/OP to accompany me to Rabat-Sale to pick up a Wimp. and take it to Cairo West. In conversation with my crew I discovered that smuggling was rife, but not so ambitious between Cairo and Morocco.

Early on the following morning we were detailed to pick up Wellington Mk XIII JA 514 at the dispersal and get airborne. I believe it was a beautiful white Wellington in Coastal Command colours. A quick check in the cockpit and I realised there were some differences – I couldn't start the thing. The crew was a bit apprehensive when I asked a fitter aboard to do it for me. A warm up and the taxying went quite well. In running up at the end of the runway prior to take-off I was puzzled to find that the pitch levers did not alter the pitch of the airscrews from fully fine and 2800 revs. Having been humiliated enough I decided to take off forthwith, confident that I could sort that matter out in the air. Lined up, I opened the throttles. Something hit me in the back of the neck and the acceleration was terrific. Surprisingly we kept to the runway and soared into the air. Throttle back, coarsen the pitch and climb. We circled and circled the airfield. I sawed the pitch levers to and fro – nothing happened. Red-faced, I was about to call the tower and ask for instructions when WO Gee said, 'My other pilots always use these switches.' Down to the left for 'Decrease' and down to the right for 'Increase'. A tentative move to 'Decrease' and the revs dropped off as the pitch coarsened! A huge sigh of relief. We were on our way to Castel Benito, via Biskra, where we night-stopped at the Hotel Atlantique, running up a bill on the imprest account.

It was a beautiful aeroplane fitted with very high-powered Hercules sleeve-valved engines. It cruised at about 190 mph, 45 mph faster than the old Ic, and at a much higher ceiling. There was a little lever, together with a new panel, which said 'Automatic pilot'. I twiddled a few knobs, lined up the artificial horizon, set the gyro and tentatively engaged the lever. It flew on its own! I could sit back. From Castel Benito it was non-stop to Cairo. Pitch alterations were made with the two switches – it obviously had electric props. It took a long time though. What were the pitch levers for? In a further examination as we approached Cairo I saw a third position for the two switches: 'Automatic', straight up! Once the switches were put there, the pitch levers operated as in the Wimpeys I had known a long time ago. A first-class landing at Cairo West and the two crew were with me.

On 3rd February we were on our way to Cairo with a Mk XIII Wellington, again via Biskra. Here I was to learn that the attraction of Biskra was not only a first-class hotel, but also that the oasis had a deprived brothel. Deprived because the only callers were a few transport and ferry pilots. If I say I did not patronise it, you may not believe me. I can only refer to my initial intent, voiced at the beginning – that this, my story, should be the truth and nothing but.

From Biskra we made 'Marble Arch' on the following day. This was a landing ground near a huge arch over a road near El Agheila. Apparently we had not damaged it as we bombed the area in January and February 1942. Story was that two thousand years before, the ruler of Benghasi and the ruler of Tripoli could not agree on the boundary between their two domains. To settle the dispute a runner was to leave Benghasi running south-west along the coast at the same time as a runner left Tripoli running south-east. Now whether someone cheated over the start, or whether a runner was nobbled, no one seems to know. Suffice it to say that when they met the Bey of Benghasi was less than pleased. The King of Tripoli had won a great slice of Cyrenaica. The Bey's unfortunate marathon runner was executed, but it was left to the invading Italians, under Mussolini, to celebrate that race by the building of this arch, nicknamed Marble Arch by the Allies. That is possibly the only untrue bit so far in this story, but my memory has not yet failed – that is what I was told, honest.

I certainly remember that night-stop, both for the discomfort and the fact that an ENSA concert was given by a Welsh concert party that night. As I remember the show was unremarkable but we did appreciate the fact that someone, somewhere had thought that those yet in the desert deserved some entertainment. It might not have been too safe for the 'Bluebell Girls'.

On 5th February we made El Adem and LG 237 in a sandstorm. There were several of us in the air looking for a place to land, and it was whilst I was on the circuit at 237 that I heard one of our Australian ferry pilots on the R/T.

'Hello Gumdrop, Hello Gumdrop, ringtwitch calling,

rrrr-ingtwitch calling. Give me a homing. Give me a homing. Out.'

'Hello aircraft, hello aircraft. Repeat your call sign. Repeat your call sign continuously.'

'Ringtwitch, ringtwitch, this is ringtwitch, ringtwitch calling, rrrr-ingtwitch calling, can't see a thing.'

'Hello Ipswich, calling Ipswich, fly 035, fly 035, fly 035. Out.'

The female radio operator had not believed her ears, or was unable to repeat the spurious call sign. I knew what the Aussie meant though. One's ring did twitch when flying haphazardly through these dust storms. I was glad to get down.

One night at Oujda, a dance had been arranged. The local belles turned up with their Mommas and Poppas to dance with the Allied Air Forces. I danced with a pretty little thing and aired my schoolboy French. She was half Arab I should think and I could not understand why she seemed to ask the same questions during different dances. I put it down to the fact that my replies were in French, too incomprehensible to understand. Despite several dances I never seemed to be able to lead successfully. At ten o'clock I saw Momma, who had gathered her family together and they were on their way home. I had been dancing with twins in complete ignorance. I bet they compared notes!

During my delivery trips I was landing as close to army hospitals as I dared, searching for my fiancée's cousin who had collected a fractured skull, as a dispatch rider. On one trip, on landing at El Aouina near Tunis, I was surprised to be instructed by an American air traffic control officer to take care, and to 'Watch out for chickens crossing the runway'. What on earth were chickens doing on the runway? On the approach I was keeping a sharp lookout, but saw no chickens. A later enquiry elicited the fact that 'chickens' was a euphemism for fighters! At breakfast the next day I was given a GI's mess tin. First I received what looked like pancakes, which were then covered with bacon. Scrambled egg was added and the whole was swiftly submerged in syrup. A pre-war breakfast absolutely spoiled. I finally caught up with Bob Lewis in hospital near Maison Blanche, the airfield for Algiers.

At about this time one flight of mine was nearly the last. On one take-off the Wimp was hard to control and when she came unstuck she went into an ever-increasing climb. All my strength was of no avail, then, just before the stall, I realised that I had taken off with 'George' engaged. A swift prayer, a flick of the switch, and WO Gee was able to collect up all the kittens that we had had. A member of the ground crew at El Adem had left the switch engaged, but my cockpit check should have discovered that fact. Cockpit checks were, from then on, more diligently performed.

And so I flew about the north African and Italian theatre, delivering these souped-up Wellingtons. The three of us delivered them, then bummed our lifts back to base at Oujda, mostly via Transport Command. One delivery of a Wellington Mk X was to Foggia in Italy via Catania. At Foggia I delivered it to my old squadron which had been taking a bit of stick over northern Italy and the Balkans. Air Commodore J.H.T. Simpson DSO, DFC, my first skipper, was the Officer Commanding 205 Bombing Group. I was not to meet him again until our first reunion after the war, where he still drank his whisky from the soup ladle we had presented to him at LG 104, El Daba. He had been confirmed then in the rank of Group Captain and eventually, as one of the most long-serving and experienced officers to survive, he was promoted to Air Commodore and given command of the Royal Observer Corps. I warrant that they did not know the calibre of their commanding officer. I believe his face and experience were too much for the establishment and so his ladle came to be used more and more, and he died prematurely in about 1954.

In late February 1944, I learned that an old school friend, F.J. Peters (Nuts Peters) was at Blida somewhere, possibly in Tunisia. Nothing for it then but to give Biskra a miss and experience a little engine malfunction to enable us to night-stop at Blida, where I found Frederick James working on the radars of No 38 Wellington Squadron of Coastal Command. The crew grumbled as the night-stop was less than comfortable, but I was able to send reassuring news to his folk and his girl back home. He was to become a lifelong friend.

On my penultimate trip to Cairo, who should I meet but 'Soda Whisky' who had been posted to BARU (British Airways Repair Unit) at Heliopolis as a test pilot. Soda took me for a test flight in a Liberator – that man could fly anything. He had an ulterior motive and suggested that I invest in some ladies' nighties and some lipsticks, talcum powder and much else, in order to transport it back to Rabat, where I would have no trouble in disposing of the contraband at a profit. I had only twenty pounds Egyptian, so Soda chipped in with another twenty. I took the risk and I was a rotten smuggler. I sweated my way up the western desert as a passenger in a Dakota. My suitcase looked brand new and obviously contained a lot more than my night-stopping kit. Undetected, I arrived back at Oujda.

On the very next day we were on our way back to Sale to collect another Wimp. My very large suitcase was more than conspicuous for such a short journey. It was even more obvious as I lugged it to the transit hotel in Rabat. Within an hour of my arrival I was in a bistro, wondering how I would find my spiv. I need not have worried. I was accosted in the loo by a little man who asked if I had 'somezing to sell'. Relieved I fetched the suitcase, handed it to my spiv, and elected to follow him to the 'boss'. Anxiously I wondered if he was on the level. Would he disappear into the Kasbah? After a ten-minute walk we arrived outside a dental surgery and inside I was to meet the Jewish dentist and his wife. They insisted on my eating a meal with them before any business. Did they know I was an amateur? The meal was not drugged and consisted of a kind of sea fish, like miniature pineapples. I don't recall how many francs we settled for but I do know that, in accordance with Soda's instructions, I asked that the money be paid in dollars. This brought in another middleman, and the dentist negotiated an exchange rate. There I was at the end of the day with over six hundred dollars and three thousand francs! My instructions were to bring men's shirts and ladies' under-clothes on the next trip.

Elated, but still apprehensive lest the SIB were waiting to pounce, we zoomed down to Cairo in Wellington Mark X, LN 984, via Oujda where I learned that I had been awarded the clasp to the Africa Star (something that the MOD subsequently denied) and I was now a Warrant Officer (temporary) and due eighty pounds in back pay. We arrived in Cairo on 13th March and I ordered my No. 1 home dress at the military tailor's in Kasr-el-Nil barracks. After all, my luck might change, and I might be posted home. There was just time to split the spoils with Soda Whisky and to fill that suitcase with shirts and ladies' undies. I do not recall whether Soda contributed.

Back we went to Oujda. This time I was more hardened. By now the authorities had forbidden the extravagant stay at Biskra, so it was back with just a call at Marble Arch and Castel Benito. At Oujda, what a calamity. I was posted as a second pilot to No 216 Dakota Squadron, the very chaps who had been flying me back to base. Now I would much rather have gone home, and I deserved it but, next to that, flying Daks from a Cairo base would have to do. To add insult to injury I was to fly my last Wimp, a Mark XIII, MF

182 back to Cairo before reporting to 216 Squadron. It was a long hard haul and took four days! To hell with it. We just had to go to Biskra for perhaps the last time. Biskra, Castel Benito, Marble Arch, El Adem and finally Cairo – it took 13 hours and 10 minutes altogether. Besides I needed time to think. What could I do with that extra suitcase which I carried along? Kitty was to find out over the next few months, as I sent parcel after parcel of shirts and odd-sized undies home. Due to censorship, I could not answer her questions as to why! The stuff didn't fit anybody – she was small but the knickers were smaller! Mail by this time took but a week between home and Cairo.

No. 216 SQUADRON AT
LG 224, CAIRO WEST

The introduction to the working office in the Dakota was quite exciting. The crew's comfort had been considered well when the C47 was born. The seats were executive class, well upholstered, with arm-rests. Even ash trays were incorporated in the furnishings. Obviously American pilots could only fly at the end of a cigar.

A Flt. Lt. Ruston showed me around the Cairo skies, the crew being a Plt. Off. Pegeus and a WO Dodgson, whose addresses I still have scribbled in my pay book. He showed me where all the popular switches and levers were and I was then detailed to the crew of WO 'Taffy' James as his co-pilot. Ruston may not have appreciated my skills. Now 'Jimmy' James was a very experienced Dak pilot. He wore the DFC as did his navigator WO Bill Gingell. Bill also had a DFM and a huge majestic moustache. The DFM was acquired as the last surviving observer in a Blenheim – or was it Fairey Battle – squadron. Quite a character. Together they had been awarded the DFC when they had been shot down whilst carrying General Ritchie's successor. They were on their way to Cairo in a Bombay. The relieving general had a short Dutch-sounding name – Gott, I think – but had he survived, Montgomery would have never drawn the short straw to take over the Eighth Army. There would have been no Lord Monty of El Alamein. He was not the first choice.

My first trip with my new crew sounds rather like a swan

around the North African haunts. Cairo West, Benina, Castel Benito, Biskra, Oujda, Rabat-Sale. We arrived on 15th April 1944 and stayed two nights in the luxurious transit hotel at Rabat. Well, three of us did. The crew took me into the Kasbah that night, where we drank beer in a bordello. The Madam sat perched on a very high stool at the bar. We sat at a table watching as the odd Free Frenchman or sailor disappeared with a selected temptress through one of the doors leading off from the bar. Some did not reappear that evening, whilst others did not stay long, but emerged with an apparent thirst, closely followed by the erstwhile companion. It came time to go, but one of our company – and I do remember his name – struck up a conversation with a pretty and shapely Franco-Arab who had only just appeared. Now our companion was almost broke, but so was the girl, because he persuaded her to let him stay the night for three British Military Pounds! The three of us returned to the hotel, more anxious for the safety of the fourth than for his morals. Might have been some envy too! However he did appear like a Cheshire cat on the morrow. The Dak was u/s. So it was down to the Kasbah, where the Cheshire cat got his face slapped for publicly airing the fact that Fatima had allowed him her favours at a cut price. Chastened and broke we made our Cook's tour return to Cairo on 17th and 18th April 1944.

On the 19th I got a lift with Flt. Lt. Ruston to Heliopolis, where I tried to find Soda. No luck. After getting back to Cairo West I was to discover that the return of a squadron aircraft from India had prompted a mess party. The prompt consisted of several two-gallon jars of Indian navy gin and Indian navy rum. The party soon got under way, and we noticed that both of the beverages dissolved the polish and the varnish from our one decent mess table. Further investigation was to reveal that both the gin and the rum were inflammable. Definitely a swift road to oblivion. The singing soon started:

141

Squadron Leaders, Wing Commanders and Group
    Captains too,
Hands in their pockets with F.A. to do,
Drinking the pay of a poor AC 2,
They're a rotten shower of bastards,
Said the airmen, Amen.

The next thing we'll pray for we'll pray for some beer,
Glorious, glorious, glorious beer,
And if we have one beer, may we also have ten,
May we have a ruddy brewery said the airmen, Amen.

Squadron Leaders, Wing Commanders and Group
    Captains too,
Hands in their pockets with F.A. to do,
Drinking the pay of a poor AC 2,
You're a rotten shower of bastards,
Said the airmen, Amen.

The next thing we'll pray for we'll pray for a bint,
Glorious, glorious, glorious bint,
And if we have one bint, may we also have ten,
May we have a ruddy brothel, said the airmen, Amen.

Squadron Leaders, Wing Commanders and Group
    Captains too . . .

The next thing we'll pray for we'll pray for a boat,
Glorious, glorious, glorious boat,
And if we have one boat may we also have ten,
May we have the bloody navy said the airmen, Amen.

Another favourite, censored a little:

Oh, the other night, when I got home, as drunk as
    drunk could be,
Saw someone's hat – upon the peg where my old hat
    should be,

So I ups to my wife and I said to her, you haven't
　　been true to me,
Whose is the hat upon the peg where my old hat
　　should be?

　She says you're drunk you nut, you silly old nut,
　　　you're as drunk as a nut could be,
　It's only a pudding bowl the neighbour lent to me.

Now a thousand miles I've travelled, a thousand miles
　　and more,
But a pudden'bowl with a hatband on, I've never seen
　　before.

Oh the other night, when I got home, as drunk as
　　drunk could be,
Saw someone's coat upon the peg where my old coat
　　should be,
So I ups to my wife and I says to her, you haven't
　　been true to me,
Whose is the coat upon the peg where my old coat
　　should be?

　She says you're drunk you nut, you silly old nut,
　　　you're as drunk as a nut could be,
　'Tis only a blanket that the neighbour lent to me.

Now a thousand miles I've travelled, a thousand miles
　　and more,
But a blanket with brass buttons on I've never seen
　　before.

Now the other night, when I got home, as drunk as
　　drunk could be,
Saw somebody's head upon the bed where my old
　　head should be,
So I ups to my wife, and I says to her, you haven't
　　been true to me,

Whose is the head upon the bed where my old head
  should be?

  She says you're drunk you nut, you silly old nut,
    You're as drunk as a nut could be,
  'Tis only a baby I have in bed with me,

Now a thousand miles I've travelled, a thousand miles
  and more,
But a baby's face with whiskers on, I've never seen
  before.

Oh the other night, as I got home, as drunk as drunk
  could be,
Saw someone's bum by my wife's bum where my old
  bum should be,
So I ups to my wife and I says to her, you haven't
  been true to me,
Whose is that bum by your old bum where my old
  bum should be?

  She says you're drunk you nut, you silly old nut,
    You're as drunk as a nut could be,
  'Tis only a pumpkin I have in bed with me;

Now a thousand miles I've travelled, a thousand miles
  and more,
But a pumpkin with an . . . .-hole in I've never seen
  before.

The final verse concerned a misapprehension about a
rolling pin, and certain appendages. I could tell someone,
but never put it into print. The party finished and I was to
wish that I could have acquired a taste for navy rum and
gin.

From 23rd to 26th April we again toured the north
African coastline, but it was on our return that I was to find

that I had been detailed to join a detachment which was going to India, to stave off the Japs, who had broken through and were at the very gates of the Raj. No way was I going, I said, and marched to the orderly room to register my protest. When Churchill visited Cairo, throwing the zobits (officers) out of the Shepherd's Hotel, and back to their desert units, he promised that no man who had completed two years in the Middle East would be posted to the Far East. My protest wasn't even considered. Churchill lightly broke his promise in my case, and amended it to 'no man who had completed *three* years'. I don't believe a trustworthy man can ever become a politician. I'm not prepared to consider that there has ever been one, nor will ever be. Honesty and politics do not gel, though politics and expediency might. Be that as it may, here I was destined for India as second pilot to the commanding officer, Wing Commander Nash, and the detachment took off on 12th May 1944.

The first stop was Habbaniya, where Harry Dawson was now a zobit. I was to get no sympathy from him. Then it was to Bahrain and Karachi, to Delhi, Allahabad and Dum Dum at Calcutta. Onwards then to a spot in the verdant jungle called Agartala. Got there on 17th May, then it was doors off and into action on 21st May. A lot of our forces were in trouble around and north of Kohima. We dropped our parachute supplies to the army at Nahemir, then back to Agartala via Jorhat and Imphal. My new skipper was a confident mad New Zealander by the name of Hirst, a flying officer.

On the following day we tried to make Imphal, on the other side of the Arakans, and in the Imphal Plain. The weather was atrocious and we couldn't get there. Our first real taste of flying through the monsoon. I note that we landed at Khum Birgram, wherever that was.

Why were we at Agartala, and what was it like? The

Japanese were making their final assault at the very gates of India and the Indo-Burmese border had been breached. Lines of communications, where they existed on either side, were made more tenuous by the jungle-clad hills and mountains. Air supply was to be the final factor in turning the tide. Our airfield was named after a small village on the edge of the verdant jungle. We lived in bamboo and palm-leaf thatched 'bashas', about a dozen to a hut. Here the punka wallahs still served to stir the hot and fetid air. When grounded by the monsoon we would stretch out on our charpoys under our mozzy nets, listening to the creak of the twenty-foot punka. Outside under a tree, on the edge of the jungle, the punka wallah would haul on the cord which pulled the palm-frond fan to and fro. As we all neared dozing, so the punka wallah would transfer the cord to his toe which he extended and retracted from a sitting position. Slowly the creaking would die away, until a raucous shout from a conscious inmate would jolt the poor wallah into action and the creaking accelerated.

It was on such an afternoon that, on the charp under the mosquito net, I slumbered covered with only a towel. Suddenly I awoke, realising that a foreign object was moving around outside the net, but resting its weight from time to time against my sweaty head. A snake, it must be, and I visualised that constrictor I had seen earlier peacefully entwined along a branch. I lay perfectly still, not daring to move or to call out. This anaconda or boa constrictor settled down, leaning against my cranium in a contented rest. My mind buzzed so hard it was a wonder it was not overheard by the snake. Now we always kept our side-arms to hand, not really for protection but because there were many light-fingered peasants around. At length I could stand the strain no more. With one swift move I sat up, grabbed my revolver and watched in amazement as a gigantic rat leapt from my pillow and dashed under the charpoys towards the doorway. I was never more frit – nor, subsequently, more relieved!

The MT Section were more educated concerning the available frills and luxuries to make life bearable, probably because they were drafted in from other RAF units in India. Be that as it may, at least one group 'bought' the services of a young girl from her peasant parents in Agartala, to be returned on departure. She dwelt amongst them without compulsion, so 'twas said, doing the dhobi, ironing, cooking and consoling!

On 23rd May 1944, with Fg. Off. Hirst as skipper, we flew to a dropping zone some forty miles east of Kohima. Much of the territory in these mountains was just a white blank on the map marked 'Unsurveyed'. After a prolonged search the appropriate markers were found in a gulley and some swadis were to be seen peering skywards. The W/Op. and the navigator went down to the rear of the Dakota, and, obeying the pilot-operated indicator lights, hurled the supplies out of the open doorway. Food, clothing, fuel and ammo. Some twiddling with the R/T set and we were in contact with the leader of the patrol. Definitely an Aussie! 'Any whisky on board, cobber?' We could only reply that there was none to our knowledge. 'When you return, cobbers, drop us a bottle or two.' They were brave men, stalking the Japs, miles from anywhere, in most inhospitable country.

Terrible weather prevented us from carrying out all the detailed sorties to the Imphal plain. My log-book reads, 'Unable to reach Imphal with reinforcements. Weather B.A.' I still didn't swear. No one ever before had needed to fly through towering cumulus clouds which could tear a kite to pieces. Air rushed about in vortices in the middle of each, at up to 200 miles per hour, it was said. Hailstones frequently damaged the Dak's skin. These towering peaks had to be pierced and prodded for a way through, by the end of the day. In the evening they began to subside. At their highest they were insurmountable. What a strange sight it was when we did get through. The Imphal plain was a billiard-table plateau surrounded by mountains, with the eastern ones full of wicked little yellow men. If that's racialism then we were all guilty.

On 31st May, as co-pilot to Sqn. Ldr. Pike, I set off for a dropping zone very close to Kohima again, just a few miles east. I had mentioned at briefing that this might very well be the patrol who had asked for whisky the week before. So two precious bottles were wrapped in clothing and fixed to a parachute. The trip was early in the morning, the sun shone and the jungle looked friendly. In our search for the drop zone we were tuned in on the R/T. It was so emotional to hear that Aussie voice. Down went the stores into their laps. All arrived safely. The final pack was most tenderly treated as we warned, 'Here comes the whisky, Digger.' I do hope that fellow made it. I'm sure the whisky helped, at least to raise morale. When we returned again to drop some more, well they really were 'Our Patrol'.

On the remaining thirteen supply drops and landings in which I took part, either drops around Kohima or reinforcements carried in to the Imphal plain, all were with Fg. Off. Hirst. Apart from the bloody weather, and the shame and frustration when we had to abort, I remember but two short incidents which made minutes of anxiety feel like an eternity of torture. After a tussle with the clouds we broke through into a sunlit Imphal plain and the skies to the east were clear. Eyes and minds were quickly focused onto a scene which included several fires, and exploding 40 mm Bofors shells. Dakotas were diving and weaving around the hillock which protected the Imphal strip. Three Zeros were, luckily for us, making off into the distance. They had pounced on our unarmed transport aircraft over the plain.

148

Thankfully we had arrived a few seconds late. I hate being unpunctual in the normal course of events. On landing we found that a Commando of the USAAF and two Daks of another squadron had bought it.

On 7th June 1944 we learned that the Japanese threat had evaporated. A return to the fleshpots of Cairo was on, so it was with some elation that we undertook the final foray. Agartala, Kangla, Jorhat, Imphal, Jorhat, Imphal and then back to Agartala. The weather was almost good, if bumpy, and on our return we came up with one of our own aircraft on the same course and height. To give Hirst his due, he was a good pilot for formation flying. I was too apprehensive of the remotely possible to be any good, and so I was in agony as the two aircraft rose and fell in the turbulence. When we flew over the lower slopes the ride became smoother, but I had kittens as Hirst manoeuvred our starboard wingtip into the open doorway of the other Dak. Petrified, I watched a crewman touch our wing from his doorway. My eye was on my parachute, and I could hardly keep my hands off it. When Hirst broke off, any grin I gave must have been very sickly.

Having carried out a swift twenty-six operational sorties inside seventeen days, we said our farewells to our borrowed ground crews and, with not the slightest regret, flew to Mahrajpur, Mauripur, Bahrain, Habbaniya and back to Cairo. At Habbaniya I shot Harry the line. We reached Cairo on 12th June where I was to discover that No. 267 Dakota Squadron, operating from Bari in Italy, required two Dakota pilots. Just think, Bari was nearer England and Kitty so, against the grain, I volunteered. At that time I believed that the alacrity with which I was accepted had nothing to do with the fact that 216 Sqadron might have been glad to see the back of me. Flying via Benina and Malta I arrived at Bari on 23rd June 1944. Here on a captured Italian airfield I joined the Flying Horse Squadron

149

and from now on I was able to contribute directly to the war effort. My luck had held.

Whilst we had been in India I received a sad letter from Jean Ackerman, to tell me that George, our W/Op. on *'ell for Leather* on 70 Squadron, had been killed in a flying accident back in the UK. A wireless operator instructor, he and Jean had lived at Stanbridge, near Leighton Buzzard in Bedfordshire. He had written to me of the 'Globe' pub on the banks of the Grand Union Canal. Four months before their baby was born, Jean had gone back to her mother's home in Blackpool. Just six weeks before the birth of Oscar George junior, his father had been flying in an Anson over the Mull of Galloway. There they had collided with another Anson on the same training exercise. All were killed, but George had been the only one to bale out. He had done so successfully before, but this time he didn't make it. I do so wish his luck had held too. He was the closest friend and confidant that I was to make whilst in uniform. He was flying from Cark, near Cartmell, after a transfer from Wing in Buckinghamshire. I was honoured to become Oscar junior's godfather.

No. 267 DAKOTA (PEGASUS) SQUADRON

Bari aerodrome was neither grass nor metalled. It was a large bare patch of compacted earth. The runway, running parallel to the not-too-distant coast, was hard and firm. The rest could be a quagmire in rain. 'We must be winning the war.' The whole field was covered with Fortresses, Lockheed Lightnings, Thunderbolts, Mustangs, Dakotas and at least one of every type that ever operated. There was even a flight of Yak fighters who, we felt, were keeping an eye on us as much as assisting Tito, who was just across the water. On one occasion we were treated to a mock dogfight between a Yak and a Mustang. All seemed pretty even, but I sensed that the Russian just had to save face, and flew beyond the plane's hairy limits. However the terminal velocity of the Mustang in a powered dive was far beyond that of the Yak so that the Mustang could break off to regain the advantage at any time. Nevertheless the Russian Air Force was something to be reckoned with for the future.

In another four months I would have been overseas for three years. Almost every few months seemed to bring some excuse for optimism concerning leave or a posting home, and I wrote to Kitty at least three times each week to learn that, rationing notwithstanding, the second wedding cake was in process of manufacture. It was inevitably to share the fate of the first – namely to serve, tier by tier, as birthday and Christmas cakes.

I was billeted in the Sergeants' Mess. a damaged, window-less barracks opposite the outdoor camp cinema, and adjacent to the Officers' Mess. Most of the glass had been blown out of the windows and the rooms did not want for fresh air. Whether the glass disappeared as a result of Allied action, or as a result of the huge explosion in Bari harbour when Jerry clobbered two ammo ships, I didn't find out. Even as the snows of winter approached our rooms were still fresh air conditioned. My cell was on the second floor, with access to the roof. There were some who had flung themselves from the high glassless windows whilst in their cups. These, if they survived, were then given the cells on the ground floor. One survived his first fall, and an intended second plunge, only to die on the third attempt.

The only alcoholic beverage was a cheap vermouth, which I blame for my current propensity for gout. Even in Italy we were obliged to take our daily dose of 'yellow perils' – anti-malarial mepacrines, or were they atebrines? The vilest-tasting non-poison that this world has ever known. The food was nothing to write home about, though I'm sure I did, but our between-flight snacks made up for any deficiencies, as we scorched round the Theatre.

Within three days of joining No. 267 Squadron I flew my first scheduled run, with a Flt. Lt. Cherry as skipper, Flt. Lt. Gilbert as navigator and Fg. Off. Landon as wireless op. Our first landing was at Foggia Main, the home of 70 Squadron, then to Naples, Cagliari and Alghero in Sardinia, and to Borgo in Corsica. We carried passengers and medical supplies, arriving at Borgo the same evening. Here the runway was again compacted earth, a strip cut through the trees, and as one landed, the ground dropped away in a steep slope. A tricky place to stick to, first bounce. There at Bevinco, Borgo's landing strip, we climbed a mountainside to a clear, freezing cold pool fed by a tumbling stream. Children were swimming in it, hardy nude little blighters.

152

As night fell, and we prepared to sleep in a ridge tent on mother earth, so the elephant-sized mosquitoes rose, squadron after squadron, and attacked. 'Now I've travelled east and I've travelled west, a thousand miles and more' but more vicious, blood-lusting aerial attackers I had never met before. (I have since – in good old England! On one afternoon in summer during the 1960s, descendants of those very same mosquitoes vanquished me in the Yorkshire Dales. I managed but one hundred yards from my car.) I could see that we were in for an exhausting night, with flailing arms waving brushwood. In desperation we filled the tent with tobacco smoke. Not the slightest effect! Then we lit a brush fire inside the tent and covered it with green grass. Success! The pungent smoke filled the tent and the mozzies could not stand it. They retreated. Unhappily we could not stand it either, and finally spent the rest of the night in the aircraft, watching the mosquitoes beating themselves to death on the windows in their endeavour to get at us. We vowed that this airfield should be in line for a delivery of mosquito nets before we returned. On the very next day, starting very early, we retraced our flights of the previous day and hit Bari that same evening. There were now 1200 hours in the log book. Many, many lucky hours.

My first operation over occupied Yugoslavia was carried out on the night of 1st/2nd July. With Plt. O Nankevill we flew into 'Piccadilly Mews' with ammunition for the partisans. There we hurriedly loaded up with wounded and took them out to Bari. Where Piccadilly Mews was I can't remember, but quite a few of us got in that night. On the night of 7th/8th July, in Dak 511, with Flt. Lt. Roberts we flew to a spot fifteen miles north-east of Ljubljaba on a supply drop. Unfortunately the drop zone was not illuminated, so we returned to base with the cargo.

On 9th July Sqn. Ldr. Noon tested a WO McDonald and me and passed us both as Dakota captains (day only!), and

I was shown around on a couple more scheduled flights before, on 27th July, I was trusted with my own crew. A very wary trio they were too. Sgt. Nicholas, who had lately recovered from a serious prang in South Africa in a Spitfire, was the co-pilot. A dapper WO Saunders (Cliff) was the navigator, and Flt. Sgt. George Telford was the sparks. They were a very quiet bunch, showing very little enthusiasm for our first venture. However, in Dakota FD 865, one of the oldest of our kites, we leapt into the air and flew through the pass to Pomigliano, an aerodrome in the shadow of Vesuvius. Fumes and smoke were still writhing from the volcano. It had recently erupted and ash had been spread around for eighty miles. Each day the sun had been obscured and ash had fallen in Bari. Pomigliano hove into view and I prayed that I might redeem myself in the eyes of this unwilling crew by not bouncing more than once. The approach was a little flat, but the air was still. Closer and closer came the tarmac as we approached from the west. Cut the throttles, hold off. Apprehension! When this Dak drops it will bounce a mile.

It floated on and on; what had happened? I suddenly realised that with airspeed at fifty-five and throttles closed we were either on the ground or on a skyhook! It had been the finest landing I had ever experienced at any time! I was subsequently to find out that this was partly because it was the smoothest, flattest runway in the world. Be that as it may, I nonchalantly taxied the kite to dispersal, noting the undeniable relief on the crew's faces, whilst trying hard to smother mine. At any rate the ice was broken, and even if I never again succeeded in landing without knowing it, the crew wouldn't be as apprehensive again; except perhaps once when Nicky leapt like a kangaroo down the runway at Elmas and I had to take her round again.

On 31st July we carried out a six-leg routine run which took in Ajaccio, and we repeated it on 1st August carrying

154

a Group Captain Musprat-Williams. Why I'm not sure. Was he checking me out for a King's Commission in the field? I think not. He did not wish to take over and fly her, but he did mildly reprimand me for wearing my Egyptian-made zobit's hat. The peak was of cardboard and cracked, and the colour was an inconsistent shade of purple in the sun and weather. Fine dust had not helped either. However I got him to Bevinco safely and was forgiven. By 15th August we had undertaken another six routine runs and I was liking the job. In my flying career to date I had landed at 97 different airfields and had flown eleven types of aircraft on eleven different flying units. The last page but one of my first flying log-book certifies that 1285 hours had been spent in the air. The very last page is proof that anyone can make a mistake. It is in red ink, and refers to gross carelessness, an endorsement authorised by the Air Commodore Commanding No. 215 Group. No one had endorsed his log-book when he broke a kite in identical circumstances!

At about this time a parcel arrived from a Mrs Mondrey in Palestine. How did she know where I was? It turned out to be a disintegrated cake; a simnel cake, or a birthday cake? The latter perhaps, some three weeks early? Perhaps Bob Mann who was still in Palestine had reminded her. But no! Unfortunately it had been posted at least a year before and was certainly inedible. It had followed me to Morocco, to Cairo, to India, back to Cairo, and thence to Bari. A much-travelled cake, and a very nice thought.

We used to walk down to the Adriatic beach on our rest days, to swim and sunbathe on the rocks. Flt. Sgts. Drew, Payne and Walton often accompanied us. They were squadron co-pilots. It was pitiful to see half-starved Italian kids plucking live jack-apple crabs from the water-covered rocks. before stuffing them alive into their mouths. It was gruesome to see a crab's leg kick as it disappeared between voracious teeth. Just outside the camp gate lived a widow, or a woman whose husband was a POW, I don't know which. However she used to do the dhobi of several of the crews and we tried to pay her well. She must have had a poorish opinion of British airmen, or of the military in general, since she used to hide her teenage daughter behind the copper on our approach. From her garden we bought small apricots at 10 lire per half kilo. The cheapest laxative ever – very gripping fruit.

On one occasion it was arranged for we Philistines to attend the opera in Bari town. The opera house was almost intact, but it was terrifying to look down at a swaying stage from the sixth-floor balcony. It was worse still when one discovered that the stage was quite stationary! I don't remember the opera, but it did cross my mind that someone could have alerted Jerry to the fact that a well-placed bomb might annihilate the personnel of quite a few Allied squadrons.

Through August and into September we flew regular routine runs around Italy, Sardinia and Corsica. Regularly we flew into Ancona and Rimini with blood for the front-line hospitals, and it was not uncommon to fly six legs in a day. On 12th September 1944, the day after I had unwisely celebrated my twenty-second birthday, Sqn. Ldr. Noon checked me out for night flying. A Fg. Off. Bramer was checked out at the same time. He too was a former Wimpey pilot. We flew around Bari harbour, not too close, and made several successful landings. At last I was a full-fledged Dak skipper. At about this time I dropped my first real para-troops near Brindisi. Cliff Saunders was delighted to be commissioned and was ecstatic to be given the job of Navigation Officer at Luqa, Malta. I've often wondered what sort of strings he had pulled. I think he was more anxious about my flying than just flying in general. For a couple of trips my navigator was Flt. Sgt. Strang, and then on 18th September, newly qualified Sgt. Sheppard, Dick, was added to my crew as my permanent navigator. Although we nearly ran into a cliffside north of Bari one foggy night, on our first night flight together, we all liked this tall, bright, young-looking fellow who fitted in and, if he felt any anxiety under pressure, didn't show it. Of course he knew that the cliff was there all the time! So for some time to come the crew was Ric, Nick, Dick and George.

At the end of September our routine runs started taking in Florence, or Firenze, where I saw first-hand the undamaged statue of David in the plaza. I shudder to think what the vandals of today might have done to Michelangelo's masterpiece. We were to fly into the island of Vis, by day, to collect badly wounded partisans. On the first occasion WO Sewell came along as an extra pilot. He was short, but a good, confident pilot who had spent the war so far as an instructor on Dakotas. He was to be awarded the DFC in Burma later. On 29th September 1944 we flew into the south of France for the first time, and routine runs took in Marseille from then on. We used to carry out two weeks of routine runs, followed by two weeks of operations over the Balkans. Each month one Dakota made a home run to Blighty and, though well down this list, I had hopes. Although junior on this squadron, I had been overseas by far the longest.

3rd October found us flying, by night, to Greece, where we took twenty fully equipped troops. Squadron Leader MacLanahan came along to check me out. I believe the landing was near Patras. The fourth of October was a red letter day, the occasion of my first solo op to the same place. Given a brand new Dakota with a two-stage supercharger, we hurtled into the night towards a mountain top near Patrai. It was 6th October, and we were to drop supplies and a couple of containers of gold sovereigns to the partisans, once we recognised the ground signals. We couldn't acquire any samples, since an untrusting army officer, armed with a drawn revolver, sat on the sovereigns! When we arrived we were somewhat puzzled since there were identical signals displayed on two neighbouring mountain tops. Jerry had put out a duplicate to confuse us. However he had chosen a mountain some 1500 feet lower, so we were able to make the correct choice. There were just two Daks on this op. The other was captained by Flt. Lt. Hall (not the hero of the song). The crew went down to the open door at the back together with the army despatcher, and round and round we circled in the dark, depositing load after load into the drop zone, grateful for the ground flares. The supplies were all dropped from three hundred feet above the target, always assuming we had set the correct barometric pressure on the altimeter. We were spot on, because we had one of those newfangled radio altimeters. We always feared night fighter interception because, with two kites in the circuit, we had to have our navigation lights on.

It is little wonder that we whistled speedily around, and made for home at a rate of knots. Imagine my dismay when I was accused by Flt. Lt. Hall at debriefing of indiscriminate supply dropping. To give the CO his due, he merely noted the complaint, choosing to await the intelligence from the partisans. It came in twenty-four hours. Every single item had landed on the very small drop zone. We didn't get an apology.

9th October dawned, and with it a flight to Brindisi. My log gives no clue as to the purpose, but a nightstop was made. On the 10th we took off for Bari and, having climbed to around two thousand feet or so I was surprised to find a Mustang formating on my port wing. The pilot, easily visible, pointed urgently downwards. What did he want? He didn't come through on the R/T at all. Still he pointed downwards, so down we went. Was it to avoid possible enemy action? We kept our eyes peeled. As we were over

158

the sea he must be suggesting that it would be safer nearer the waves, so nearer we went. There he was, still on our wing tip and still pointing downwards. The man was mad, I couldn't go much lower. Notwithstanding, we seemed to fly through the spume of the wave tops. My erstwhile escort disappeared. We sped on at just above the waves when, just ahead, an Italian fishing smack appeared. Our approach was spotted by the crew at the last moment. They surely wondered 'friend or foe'. Lower still we went until, just before reaching the boat we eased up over the mast, looking back to see the ashen faces of the crew who lay on their backs looking upwards. We just missed the mast top. Then I saw it! In my backwards glance I saw that the port undercarriage was down! So that was what the Mustang pilot had been trying to tell us. We had missed that mast by some four feet less than I thought. Somewhat humbled, I reduced speed in a climb and managed to retract the recalcitrant wheel. I implored the crew to keep this misdemeanour quiet.

Three days later, once again in one of our newest Dakotas, we set off at night to scatter sovereigns and ammo around. The target was well inland, near a place I have recorded as Koritza. The met forecast was bad, and as we neared the Yugoslavian coast we could see great flashes of lightning ahead, illuminating masses of towering cumulonimbus clouds. Not deterred, we climbed up and up, using oxygen from 11,000 feet onwards. Higher and higher the beast went, sometimes changing course to avoid the towering cloud peaks. The radio was soon useless. Press on regardless. Far below lightning frizzled across the sky, between the invisible mountain tops; an eerie picture. Not much fear of interception. Up and up we climbed into the starlit but moonless blackness. Perhaps Koritza would be clear, although we knew that a successful outcome would be difficult. There we were at 24,500 feet, with just a few cloud peaks to avoid, almost in the clear. On and on, hanging on the props. Press on! Despite the weather we would not let Tito down (though my earlier sympathies were with Mihailevitch). Then it happened. Almost at the drop zone, by dead reckoning, the stars started to go out, as did my ultraviolet-lit instruments. I was going blind. Realising that I was about to pass out I said, 'Take her, Nick,' as I fell forward in my seat. I don't know what degree of panic set in with Dick and George. The latter told me later that he would have taken Nicky out of the pilot's seat and would have landed it himself, since Nick hadn't yet landed by day, let alone in darkness. My wager would have been that there our glorious partnership would have ended. Whether we would have survived or not we shall never know, because the cockpit lights gradually came on again and the stars appeared. We were on a reciprocal course. I sat up. 'I've got her Nick.' In searching for an explanation we surmised that I had put my elbow on my oxygen tube, squashing it. Now everyone knows that survival is more than difficult without oxygen. My recovery was due to my collapse – I fell off the tube! This time I could not persuade the crew that they keep our secret. Within hours of our safe return, after an abortive attempt, the whole squadron had a good laugh. I warrant that they ensured a clear oxygen line for themselves thereafter.

One of our WO crews, with much experience, set out on a night mission from one of the most northerly Allied airfields in Italy, to fly into a secret field in Poland to bring out some Polish partisan, or free government leaders. The Dak had to land in Poland under Jerry's nose. We knew nothing of this until more than a month later, when the crew reappeared. The skipper was now a Pilot Officer with a brand new DFC. I found myself envying him his flight from Poland on to Blighty and his lengthy leave the most. They had endured three weeks in rationed, wartime England. Lucky buggers. Oh! I forgot – I did swear occasionally now.

In a few more days it would be three years since I had seen Kitty or my family, and I would have welcomed the chance to try my luck on such a mission. I was absolutely sure that Kitty would wait out whatever time was required, but it was disconcerting, nevertheless, to see the increasing number of 'Mespots' which were stuck to the mess notice board. Mess members added their own comments about the lady to the exposed letter, before it was returned to the unfaithful writer. When a squadron member got a 'Dear John Mespot' from his girlfriend or wife, to break the news that she was pregnant by, living with, or marrying someone else, it was easy to share his grief and frustration. He could only pour his heart out to his friends. The friends would supply the deadening grape, write less than complimentary remarks on the letter, and return it to its source. The term Mespot originated from pre-war days when unaccompanied husbands in Mesopotamia frequently heard news of their partners' infidelity.

The whole squadron was briefed for a daylight on Bucharest on 1st November 1944. The Germans were supposed to have pulled out and I believe that the operation involved taking in food and medical supplies and advisers, and bringing out certain officials more sympathetic to the West than to the Russians. Eighteen Dakotas were set to go. However on the eve of the op my crew was stood down. Another emergency had arisen and our aircraft was to proceed to Kalamaki, an Athens airport, on a detachment of some length, attached to Air Headquarters, which was still ship-bound off the coast. The next day, after a three-hour flight, we landed at Kalamaki. We were billeted in the Hotel Spendide, where the rooms were freezing, the beds were comfortable, and the food was boiled tinned potatoes and bully beef, or bully beef and boiled tinned potatoes. We were to be briefed daily at the hotel.

Our instructions on 3rd November were to find a clandestine airfield known as Piccadilly Pearl, to land and hand over our cargo to whomsoever we found in charge. We took off early and, after one and a half hours, we had discovered what we thought to be the place, still locked in the morning mist. A search disclosed a large village two miles away. The airfield was deserted and inhospitable. After circling for a while we spotted a truck moving out from the village and proceeding towards the field. Might be Jerry, so we climbed a bit. The long-forgotten recognition signal was given as the truck reached the field and in we went. We were welcomed by a lot of bearded cut-throats, led by a suave English army captain, dressed most improperly. We buckled to to unload the stores, the captain searching for the non-existent beer. He implored me to bring him some on my next visit, and to that end he gave me a sovereign from a heavy little leather bag attached to his belt. So a few of our sovereigns had reached proper hands. Each was worth £25 in Athens and the boot boys had a bag full each! It would buy a lot of beer in Athens.

Off we went back to Kalamaki and on the same day we transported an RAF Unit with tents, rations, generator and radio sets to Sedes, near Salonika, where they were to set up an airfield control. Now Sedes was just a strip in a field, marked by little flags, and we were warned to stay within those flags at all costs. The enemy had mined the field on their retreat, and only a twenty-five yard wide strip had been cleared. We overflew the retreating Jerries, and the Allied invasion fleet anchored in the bay. Feeling like the drunk who had safely walked the chalk line, and wiping the sweat from our sticky hands and brows, we unstuck our trousers from our clinging bottoms. Reception was a small mine-clearance party. With the airfield control party

162

unloaded it was up and back to Athens, after pleading with the mine clearers to give us an extra few yards for the morrow. Back in Athens we were to discover that we were to fly twice a day, or more, between Tatoi, another Athens aerodrome, and Salonika. We also found that inflation in Athens was of the runaway Deutschmark type of post Great War years, no doubt exacerbated by the number of gold sovereigns there were around.

That evening I changed a one pound sterling British Military currency note with a kerbside money changer. He gave me all the drachma notes that he had. Hundreds of two thousand million drachma notes! I crammed the notes into my breast pocket and the huge knee pocket of my battledress, and George and I decided to go to the pictures. On the way we noticed that street traders were selling tins of bully and New Zealand butter, NAAFI issued cigarettes and other rations. The butter I recall was the equivalent of £2/10/- a pound! Where did they get it? Who was the crook making the money? Army, navy or air force? As we went into the foyer of the cinema we noticed that Mr Greek was buying just two cigarettes from a spiv with a tray before he entered the cinema. Some bought only one. Billions of drachmae changed hands. The cinema cashier took all the notes I had in my large pocket before we were waved into the cinema. It must have cost upwards of a light year in drachmae to get in. What we saw I know not. The show over, I ordered two beers at a pavement bistro. Came the beers and I proffered the rest of my notes. He took all the notes, and one of the beers – George and I shared the other!

On 4th November we made two trips to Salonika, transporting three jeeps, three zobits, a generator and an FFCU, whatever that was. We made similar trips on 5th and 6th November. On the 7th we had a day off and were shown around the Acropolis by the wife of a pre-war Greek cabinet minister by the name of Landos. She introduced us to her son, a Free Greek naval commander who had come ashore from the invasion fleet.

On our daily trips to Tatoi by bus we met a young girl, whose name escapes me, and an older woman by the name of Cleo, who spoke several languages, including English. The elder was very attractive and protective of the younger. We did no more than speak with them, persuading them to be photographed with us. Cleo was the Tatoi interpreter and she asked if, on our return to Italy, we would purchase some nylons for her. 'Nylons' had to be explained to us. Stockings had either been silk or lisle when we left Blighty. We never did carry out her request. Apparently Cleo had been an interpreter for the Germans before we arrived, and we were later to learn that she had been executed in a particularly vicious and messy way by the Communist partisans. Can't remember if they were EAM or ELAS. Together those partisans were later to capture the whole of our SHQ and march them off into the mountains, holding them to ransom. Luckily it was after our departure.

On one of our trips to Salonika we were asked by the newly set up Air Traffic Control to buy them some drachmae in Athens. We bought them a bucketful for a couple of pounds. They bought a dozen eggs for just a few hundred drachmae, confirming that inflation hadn't hit Salonika to the same extent. Daily we plied between Athens and Salonika taking petrol, provisions and kitchen sinks. Arriving at Tatoi one day we were to find that our friend the Greek lieutenant commander was due to fly up with us. He was accompanied by two huge suitcases. In trying to load them, one of us pulled off a handle disclosing that one case at least was full of drachmae! The other was just as heavy – billions and billions of newly printed drachmae. We thought we knew what he was up to, but took him to Salonika with his loot, as ordered. He must have bought up half the city for a few quid.

This may explain why, on a later trip, I was confronted at Salonika by a small party led by a man who claimed to be a director of the Royal Bank of Greece. He was agitated about entrepreneurs who were buying up real estate with what would soon be worthless paper money. Would I please take him to Athens? I explained that without authority from the British Military Authorities sitting aboard ship in the bay, I dared not. He said he would make it well worth my while. He must have cursed that honesty was foiling him and helping the crooks, and he had my sympathy. Imagine my chagrin on the following day when I was instructed to bring him and his entourage to Athens, for nothing. A case of honesty not paying, I thought. I knew then I was destined to remain poor. I never saw Mrs Landos or her son again.

On 11th November we were returning to Tatoi after our first flight to Sedes that day when we discovered that we had no hydraulic pressure. The undercart would not come down and lock. Calamity! We circled, trying with the hand pump to get the wheels to lock down, to no avail. The hydraulic tank was almost empty. There had been a leak. What could we do? Whilst frantically operating the hand pump we emptied our coffee into the tank. Nick pumped whilst we all had a leak which joined the coffee. Eureka! Coffee and urine had got us out of the proverbial! After landing we explained what had happened to the riggers, whose job it was to flush out the system. They said they were pissed off, and we sympathised. A rigger had once served me a dirty trick on 70 Squadron when he had blocked up the wee-wee tube as it left the aircraft. This had left me wondering what to do with a funnel full of urine in the left hand whilst the right hand was forming a pincer movement. Now I had my revenge by proxy.

The end of our detachment came on 15th November. From Tatoi we flew a brigadier and his five staff to Rome, where I fell foul of an Anglophobic Yankee colonel who was the commanding officer at Ciampino. He was irate to find that the clouds of dust blowing in through his office window had been caused by an English non-commissioned officer, flying a lease-lend American C 47. Threatened with a court-martial I was very diplomatic, filled with phoney remorse. I felt I had to be. He wore his forty-five belligerently in an open holster like Buck Jones. What a nut! I did report the incident to my CO, together with the report of our detachment in Greece, but nothing more was heard.

We discovered that the squadron had had a shaky do over Bucharest. They had to let down blind through 10/10 cloud over the valley. They relied for the first time on a newish radar location system which wasn't too reliable in the Balkans. Luckily no one was lost in the descent, but some had to abort. I much preferred the 14 days we had spent in Greece. I never did get back to Picadilly Pearl with beer for the army liaison officer, so I blew the sovereign, together with a tin of bully, and bought an accordion. That instrument was thereafter used to accompany such songs as would be censored here. Songs that referred to a famous tinker, or to a certain ship named after the Goddess of Love. The accordion is still in the loft, in pieces.

On one occasion at a mess binge I met Flt. Sgt. Gelbauer, a Pole who had been a pilot at Comm. Flight, Iraq. He was now serving on a rocket-firing Hurricane Squadron. Their targets were usually ships, and he painted a hairy picture of pilots blowing themselves up with their own rockets as they followed them down into the target. The philosophy came to be fire and immediately break off. I mention Gelbauer as a sort of talisman of mine. He did survive. I was to meet him as a Flight Lieutenant on a troop ship in Aden in 1959, as he was on his way to fly spotter planes in Malaya.

166

At a mess party the young and not so young ladies of the environs turned up with their mommas. I don't recall dancing, though no doubt I did. The SNCOs were anticipating a great time when the covers were removed from a delicious-looking buffet spread on an old billiard table. Chaperoning mommas forgot their daughters in the rush. None of us could get near the food which was rapidly swept into the doggy bags brought by the mommas. Sausages by the score, ham sandwiches, cheese rolls and fruit were swept away by the forearm full. In one minute there was nothing to see but crumbs and empty dishes. In eye-glazed amazement we watched as the mommas gathered up their daughters and made an immediate retreat down the approach road to the town. They didn't wait for their buses. Most of us were hurt because the food was as appetising to us, and some because other fruits had been plucked from them. Wherever the hurt was felt, and however long it lingered, no party was ever arranged again. Our only contact with the Italians from then on was with the dhobi lady and with the driver of a small-gauge steam railway engine which passed our barracks twice a day. In exchange for a few cigarettes he would throw lumps of coal from the engine for us. With the bitter winds and early snow, the coal was welcome.

On a routine run to Ancona and Pescara we were to see a flame-throwing tank incinerate the occupants of a huge farmhouse. The yards of flame went into one window and issued forth from every other. What a terrible weapon it was. At Pescara, or was it Ancona, a strange sight greeted us. On landing we noticed a Fortress on its belly just off the end of the runway. We enquired whether any US airmen were hurt in the prang, which was covered in foam. The reply was quite amazing. The aerodrome control staff had watched the Fortress descending from the north in line with the runway. They fired red Verey lights since the undercarriage was retracted. Steadily the plane descended, grounding just off the centre of the runway. The fire crew were alongside with foam almost as soon as the kite had stopped. Was anyone hurt? 'We don't know,' was the reply. 'There was no one on board!' Had they baled out over a northern target?

A return flight to Bari on one occasion found the field in an almost unusable condition. It was a quagmire of mud and slush. Landing was straightforward enough, just a little more surface water than usual. Taxying was difficult if not quite impossible and an attempt saw my starboard wing slide behind the fin of a Fortress. The rudder was badly damaged in the collision, but even the nav. light cover survived on the Dak. Again I was for the high jump and the USAAF colonel was in high dudgeon. My guilt was obvious, and I recalled that the American officers demoted their men almost at a whim. Came the day of the decision and the Yank withdrew the charges. Apparently my collision disclosed that an important modification to the Fortress rudder had been overlooked, and the incident was swept quietly under the partial carpet. Wing Commander Francombe's eyes twinkled as he told me of my escape.

One of the liaison officers operating with the partisans turned out to be an RAF Sergeant who had been a parachute instructor with 4 METS and the Long Range Desert Group. I cannot recall his name, but I know he survived the war and emigrated to Canada. He was now a pilot officer with extremely poor eyesight. He was difficult to understand, especially when in his cups, as he was a broad-speaking Scot. On one occasion when I was due to land him at a partisan airfield, we noted that there were two runways lit, and two identical sets of identification lights. How to decide where to land? Which was the mock-up by Jerry? Plt. Off. 'Jock' insisted on baling out over the suspected correct strip. He would fire an illuminating cartridge if our reasoning was correct. No time to consider what might happen if we were incorrect! We circled in anticipation without attracting ground fire. At long last there came the signal, so in we went to meet up with a grinning Scot, to unload the supplies and to pick up the casualties. 'Jock' stayed behind with the partisans as we ran up on the brakes and roared away into a steep climbing turn out of the valley. Jock, I recall, had been a friend of Army Warrant Officer Dawes, the most senior instructor at Kabret.

A week or so later Jock was picked up by another aircraft and reappeared in Bari. He was again delivered to a spot in Yugo which required that he had to bale out, since there was no strip. The story went, and I believed it, that he used to hide up in a pub, wherein he had a girlfriend. The pub was well patronised by the Wehrmacht and he came and went via the windows. I know no more, but I wish he would tell his story. He had no nerves, no fear and always carried a knife. I'm positive he used it well. Unfortunately he was put out of action as he sped round the Officers' Mess on a miniature paratroop motorcycle. Apparently he made for the door, missed it and hit the wall. He broke a limb and was *hors de combat* for weeks.

We left Ancona for Naples on 28th November 1944. The weather worsened and a few miles out from Naples we ran into pouring rain, hail and low heavy clouds with very poor visibility. There was no hope that we might make Pomigliano, under Vesuvius, nor could we see Naples. In following the coastal motorway southwards we spotted an airfield running east to west. We had not seen it before and our maps did not show it, but we dared not lose it in that weather. With hindsight I think I should have stood off out at sea, but a circuit or two and I decided that we must go in. Almost blinded by rain, we hauled ourselves low over the boundary and dropped in, literally, stopping in a very short distance – made it yet again! Dick called my attention to a Mitchell following up close behind. He must have thought it was his lucky day too. Swiftly we were off the runway onto a muddy taxi track. The Mitchell needed a lot more room and shot by to end in a drainage ditch with damage to his nosewheel. Together the two crews, each of which thought that the other knew where it was, sloshed their way to a few EPIPs. There we surprised an RE captain supping beer with a couple of NCOs. Out in the wilds in the midst of a storm they hadn't expected anyone, nor had they heard us land. They were incredulous at our story, especially since the strip had been out of use since they had removed the linked metal cladding which had covered the runway! The ground underneath should not have supported us, besides it was littered with drainage channels. Quoth the Mitchell skipper, 'I know.' I think he blamed me for leading him astray. The airstrip had been known as St Maria. After two hours of steady drinking we tried and were successful in contacting Capodichino and awaited our collection. The beer was free and had been the rations for a company of Engineers. However they were all Sikhs, and quite teetotal. We envied British officers and NCOs in charge of such obliging troops.

On the following day we returned to pick up our Dak, after reconnoitring a drain-free strip. Taking off without mishap we made Pomigliano, stayed the night and rested. We made Bari on the following day with nine American women soldiers as ballast, after flying all round the toe of Italy, since the passes were still closed by threatening weather. With this pleasant and surprising company we didn't mind the detour, though at times the girls were a little breathless, through lack of oxygen at altitude. The crew didn't mind sharing their masks. We were very popular with the Yankee contingent at Bari for delivering this feminine company to them. I believe they were nurses.

December was spent on operations to various Greek destinations. It was then that we learned of Cleo's demise.

On one such trip to Athens we carried an official photographer who photographed the whole of the Pegasus Squadron in formation over the Gulf of Corinth. On another trip, returning from Hasani, we had to fly westwards along the Gulf of Corinth in blinding snowstorms. The Gulf of Corinth was several miles wide and lay between two ranges of mountains, but we were soon bathed in sweat, having to entrust our lives to an inaccurate compass and its interplay with the earth's magnetic field. Visibility in driving snow is measured in yards. I'm sure that had we hit a mountain we would only have seen it just a split second before, as we peered ahead. In snow we crossed the Adriatic, and in snow we landed at Bari. All this ring-twitching hassle to deliver Keatings powder and toilet rolls, four tons of the stuff. What a war!

It was in December too, and in a slight snowstorm that, peering from our unglazed barrack room window, George said, 'Here comes the CO.'

'How do you know?' I asked.

'Well that's the CO's jeep,' quoth George. 'See the number?'

I admitted to being able to see the jeep, so off to the quack I was pushed for a sight test. The result? 6/9 with each eye whatever that meant. Probably a nice safe little ground job, preferably at home? No such luck. With the proverbial steel-rimmed issue specs, I could see 6/5 and that meant better than I ever had before. I could see the instruments quite clearly! On 27th December I tried landing at Brindisi with my specs on. Everything was crystal clear on the approach. This would be a peach of a landing. Hold off, hold off, float, float, float. Nerve gone I pushed up my specs, only to find that I was still fifteen feet up! Back I went to feeling for the ground.

The few days following 25th January 1945 were very interesting and exciting indeed. Really it all started with a routine run on 24th January, in one of our veteran Dakotas, FD 965. The theatre of operations had enlarged, so that this trip was a new one for what was now an all warrant officer crew. From Bari to Catania to Pomigliano to Ciampino, then a night-stop. Then Borgo, Marseille, Borgo, Ciampino. Again a night-stop. The mechanics of the trip were all forgotten, save on the leg Ciampino to Borgo. Clouds were low, a little more than 1000 feet, and very dense. Passengers were staff and 'swanning' officers. Flying just below cloud, halfway across the Corsican Sea, I happened to glance back over the port engine to see a radial engined FW 190 making a beam attack. I never acted quicker; straight into a steep port slipping turn. I watched the FW 190 speed by astern. It was a USAAF Thunderbolt, which was no consolation to the zobits who were picking themselves off the floor in the passenger cabin. Better a scared officer than a dead one. My apologies were not well received. Surely I could recognise a friend? Given time, sure I could. The toilet was well patronised for the rest of the flight.

After the second night-stop we had but Pomigliano, Catania and Bari to make on 26th January. We got only to Pomigliano in the shadow of Vesuvius. In approaching the terminus we passed a dozen Blighty-marked brand new Dakotas. At debriefing we were told that our aircraft was to be commandeered, since one of the dozen visitors, on a secret trip, was unserviceable. Disconsolate we just sat around envying the forty-eight smartly dressed officers who had just brought in the Daks from Blighty. Where was that place? Would we ever see it? Now whether it was our wreck of an ancient C 47, or whether our CO had signalled 'Nuts. If you want my kite you must take Barfoot and the crew as well,' I'm not really sure, but knowing Wing Commander Francombe I like to think it was the latter. Our kite was loaded with flares, generators and air traffic control equipment from the U/S Blighty Dak, and we were briefed to make Hasani in Greece that night. The other eleven officer-manned super Daks disappeared ahead as old FD 965 lumbered along into the gathering dusk. Needless to say we landed at Hasani too late to see the going of the Blighty crews in their No 1 home dress.

Given three blankets and an area of concrete floor we attempted rest. We literally froze and every joint seized. We sat up smoking for most of the night and reported early to the Intelligence Section. There we sat around waiting for the forty-four zobits. 'All the fours, Pompey ladies,' said George. When they arrived they gave us a wide berth. Four scruffy warrant officers in khaki battledresses, filthy and no doubt smelly too. At briefing we learned our destination; a place called Saki in the Crimea. Russia by gad! Off we all took, and once again the eleven disappeared into the distance. No thought of a convoy for the poor old Pegasus. Warned to avoid Turkey we chugged on, saw the Bosphorus, and sped at 145 miles per hour across the Black Sea. Through threatening skies and snowstorms we ploughed on dead reckoning. Good old Dick, we had flown his courses well and we hit Saki or thereabouts right on the nose. The runway was clear of snow and in we went to be guided by a fur-clad bod to dispersal. Whilst the kite was being unloaded, a wreck of a bowser, seemingly a three-ton truck with an unbaffled tank on, drove up to dispersal and refuelled us with the minimum for a return to Hasani. How that bowser coped with the slush, snow and mud I'll never know, since our sophisticated, purpose-built tankers would have failed. I noticed the zobits, in a large heap, were persuading a wing commander liaison officer that the weather was too bad for an immediate return to Greece. They stayed, as did we. A couple of battered buses took us through the gates of what we later found to be a sanatorium, inside a large barbed wire compound.

We four WOs were led independently by a large Russian

bird down a very, very hot corridor, past furnace doors located in the walls, to a room containing four cots. It must have been 130 degrees in that room! The walls were almost too hot to touch. We started to strip off both for comfort and to make use of the buckets of warm water and the wash-hand stands. George, always one to go to extremes and being quantitatively well endowed, stood by his cot in his birthday suit. I made my way a little more demurely to the basin. Phew! We said it was too bloody hot. Suddenly the door opened and in came our erstwhile escort. She was six feet tall, carrying a small axe, and she made in the direction of George. Even he wilted as he attempted to protect his equipment with his hands. Olga brushed past him, axe in hand, and nailed a black-out screen to the window with the back of the axe. Not a word, and she turned to leave the room. A shattered and perspiring George fell onto his cot, thankful for his narrow escape. Olga and George still had their choppers.

Washed and brushed up we were guided to a dining room to be served by buxom Russkis with all kinds of unrecognisable grub. Certainly it was obvious that we were being spoiled. A pity that the fish was raw; at least I assumed it was fish. The bread was black, and the grease was goats' butter, I think. The Russian peasants saw very little food like that but we felt that we daren't leave any. The best part of the meal was the little glass at the right elbow. It was filled with Vodka. I drank mine; Dick didn't like it so I drank his. No sooner was a glass empty than it was refilled ... both of them. It took a little longer to empty this time, but then again they were refilled. What the lads did that night I don't know, as an excess of grain spirit put me to sleep and I didn't notice the heat. Apparently the others slept poorly, interrupted frequently by Olga who was always opening the furnace doors and, after hurling in a few logs, clanging them shut. The fire was inside the hollow walls, Roman-fashion.

On the next day there was much more snow and though the Russkis wanted us away, we stayed. An American top sergeant attached to some diplomatic staff sold us an almost worthless Russian currency note. It wouldn't buy anything. We walked the wire watching the sentries. Then we saw two little boys, about ten years old, outside the fence. They were lightly clad, looked frozen and wore straw boots. George and I made snowballs and soon we were laughing with the kids and enjoying ourselves. Came a bellow and a burly Russian sentry chased the kids off with the flat of his bayonet. Obviously the kids were not to fraternise – my first close-up of the Russian attitude. More was to follow. We were given another good but uncooked meal that night and this time I kept to my own Vodka glass and left a little in it. We learned from the Yank that the Black Sea Fleet were to lay on a concert of song and dance for us, in a small hall. Along we went to arrive first. We selected seats halfway back from the stage and watched the Russian soldiery, airmen and sailors who drifted around. The forty-four zobits of the Royal Air Force arrived and promptly filled up the first two rows of chairs. I remember thinking how honoured they must feel to have been allocated such seats. I couldn't have been more wrong. A wicked-looking cut-throat of a Mongolian officer strode in, saw the situation and strode out again. After a few moments he returned with a giant of a man, fully seven feet six inches in his Astrakhan hat, accompanied by a slender glamorous woman. He marched to the front, his English was limited, eyed the Royal Air Force for a moment then barked an order which could not be misinterpreted. Pointing to the back he said 'Out'. We grinned as they sheepishly filed into the seats behind us. The concert was not in our honour, I guess, because only then did the Russians pour into the auditorium and fill up the rest of the seats, from the front. There was energetic dancing, some Volga boatmen singing and some balalaika and accordion playing. I understood none of the repartée, though we joined in the clapping. The music was excellent. All eyes occasionally turned to the Commissar's lady, so different from the hard-working camp women. She deigned no one a glance. She dared not. Another hot night was to follow though it snowed outside. On the following day it was blowing a gale but this time the Wing Commander lost the argument and we had to leave for Bari, via Hasani. It was impressed upon me that we should tell no one of this expedition.

Old FD 965 started easily and we were the first to get airborne, glad to be on our way. West sou-west we headed under scudding but brightening clouds. With almost 150 on the clock and the rest of the fleet passing us, Dick soon worked out that we were heading into a sixty miles per hour wind. Progress was very slow. Not only were we wary not to overfly Turkey but our fuel gauges gave us cause to worry. We had been allowed the minimum at Saki, so it was considered that we might see the war out in the safety of some Turkish harem. On and on we droned, turning left somewhere north of Salonika. The ground went by even more slowly, so that we did wonder whether sea or rough land might be the best place in the case of the gravy running out. At Salonika we decided we could make it. Rings twitched but with the proverbial pint left in the tanks we dragged ourselves onto the runway at Hasani. The flight that outwards had taken four hours and fifty minutes had taken six hours and forty-five minutes on the return. We arrived fifty minutes after the UK squadron and once again found that no one expected us. However we insisted on better accommodation than we had had three nights earlier. On 30th January we took off for Bari. The rest went back to Blighty via Pomigliano.

Back at Bari we were greeted by the reception crew with 'The squadron is off to Burma'. Hell no! I had only selected the vacancy in 267 Squadron since 216 Squadron had been sending detachments all over the option. Confident that with three years and three months overseas, nine months of which should count time and a half for service in Paiforce and down the Gulf, I would soon be going home, I wouldn't have demurred if Kit had set about making another cake. With the equivalent of three years and seven and a half months of overseas service, Winston Spencer Churchill would keep his amended word. I was already sorry for my crew who hardly had their knees brown. The orderly room was informed of my expectation to remain behind as the squadron set out for the Far East. Hearing of this, the CO sent for me and, after prising from me where we had been for the past week, he assured me there was nothing in writing to prevent me from tackling the Japanese. Damn Churchill. Was the man's word never to be honoured? It was supposed to be in AMOs wasn't it? No one could find it and I searched the dog-eared, incomplete, squadron copies most carefully. How the heck could a chap be expected to survive this war, if he had to go on to the next, and the next? I felt that the only folk on my side were the present and future relatives of mine. However we now had but three days to prepare. Preparations included the issue of small arms again, but I was so late that I could only obtain a 1918 Webley forty-five, which was U/S on one chamber. They could only give me eleven rounds. Look out the Japanese!

Somewhat later in February I was to realise that our trip to the Crimea had been in preparation for the Yalta Conference, where we sold out Europe . . . or half of it.

On 3rd February 1945 we took off for El Adem, as a squadron, en route for the South East Asia Command.

BURMA: HERE WE COME

We arrived in Cairo in KG 523 on 3rd February having refuelled at the first airfield I had bombed in the Middle East over three years before, El Adem. In Cairo erstwhile comrades of 216 Squadron offered no sympathy. After all they had been to the Far East once before, as I well knew, to Agartala and to Imphal. It was only fair and just that 267 Squadron should take its turn now, wasn't it? After all we were both squadrons of No 216 Group and they were senior, weren't they?

In Cairo we stayed for three days collecting ground equipment, stores, provisions and spares for our imminent departure. On 6th February we flew to Shaibah, and on the 7th we reached Karachi via Bahrain. On the 8th the destination was Bilaspur. I've no idea now where it was, but suffice it to say that it was a brand new flying station opened to receive us.

We were grounded in Bilaspur for two weeks and I cannot remember how we passed the time. From the first night however, the termites could be heard attacking the roof trusses in the ceilings of the new quarters and in the mess. In seeking an explanation for the abrasive grinding sounds which went on all night, we discovered that three de Havilland Mosquito aircraft had been rendered useless by these voracious termites. Their tail-planes had been eaten into a very weak state. The plywood, from that time on, had

178

to be specially treated in Canada before the wooden aircraft, the pride of the Allies, could be built and shipped to India.

After a few days roofs started collapsing all around the camp. Luckily ours did not, but we had to be ready to bale out at any time. The mess was luxury indeed. Turbaned waiters pandered to us whilst we built up our strength. My one and only visit to the town of Bilaspur left just one abiding memory. I was solicited by a boy of about ten years and, upon my refusal, he offered me his little sister. Poverty was the sole cause of their misfortune. Poor little devils.

On 22nd February 1945 we flew a cargo to Tulihal, an airfield a few miles south of Imphal on the plateau. Upon our return the squadron packed and set off to take up residence there. We shared Tulihal with a Canadian squadron of Dakotas. No mess had been built and there were only a few bashas completed. I was CMC of the non-existent mess. We collected our food from the kitchen and, if we could evade the ever-vigilant kite hawks, we returned to our billets to eat it. On the very first occasion I lost my bully to a kite which zoomed over my shoulder and grabbed the meat in its talons. It left boiled potatoes, onions and haricot beans undisturbed. From then on we protected our rations with the newly issued bush hats.

Three days after arrival Fg. Off. Baker and his co-pilot, WO Gulliver, Nicky and I flew to Kumbirgram and onwards to Lallaghat to practice the towing of gliders. For what reason we were never to know. I assume that the aircraft we flew was a borrowed 'special' fitted with towing gear, since I never flew it again. After verbal instruction we trundled down the long runway with a WAACO in tow. The glider was quickly airborne but we came unstuck with only two hundred yards to go. A short stooge around at reduced knots and the glider released himself over the airfield. I can't remember whether we dropped the towline or wound it in. Then someone suggested that we try two gliders. I was really worried but was assured that this was common practice in the UK. The hell it was! A much, much longer trundle began, at full boost with overdrive. I was to try it first, whether it was because of my experience or my lower rank, I was not quite sure. We threw in the extra horses and held the kite down until the last foot of runway. Airspeed was probably too low. Since there was no chance to abort I did not look at the ASI but very gently eased the stick back and we skimmed the stunted trees at the edge of the airfield. With courage I had bravely decided that if we started to slip into the woods the gliders would have to be sacrificed, released to fend for themselves. Flat out we gained inch after inch, clawing our way into the sky. Skimming the endless trees at a worrying eighty miles per hour we wondered how this exercise would terminate. The two glider pilots were either just as petrified or very ignorant. I'm sure now that the ground must have dropped away and, after a wide sweep of fully half an hour, we manoeuvred over the drome at two hundred feet. In case the glider pilots were not prepared to go, we gave them no option, pulling the release with relief. We watched their bumpy but safe arrival. On landing I gently pointed out the imbecility of towing two gliders with a clapped-out Dak from an airfield way above sea level. Fg. Off. Baker declined his turn and I vowed never again. Those two gliders weren't even loaded.

Five days later, bereft of cargo doors, we started the Pegasus Squadron's support of the army's gruelling advance. The first sortie was a landing with men and supplies at Sinthe, an advanced landing ground. Before landing we saw a few gliders on the ground and most were burning. They had only been released that morning and had landed safely only to be attacked by Zeros of the Imperial Japanese Air Force. Perhaps it had been intended for us to take part in that operation. Presumably the Zeros were from Rangoon or Moulmein. It wasn't going to be a party after all, especially since most of our flying was to be in daylight. Bad weather was to become our worst enemy and our best friend, since it kept the Jap fighters grounded.

The sight of the Arakans and the jungles was not new to me, but it filled Nick and Dick and George with awe. They were to be the despatchers, by the open doorway, during the manoeuvres for supply drops. From now on survival was the name of the game. Later that same day we dropped a load of ammunition over Kamye. Thereafter operations seemed to take place on every other day: on the 4th, 6th, 8th, 10th, 12th, 14th, 16th and 18th March. Perhaps a Sunday intervened because the logbook then reads 21st, 23rd, 25th, 27th, 29th, and so it went on, two or three sorties each day. Respite was supposed to come after 600 operational hours over the most inhospitable region in the world in the worst of monsoon weather. Six bloody hundred hours! The powers that be did say 'or 150 sorties, whichever came first'. You had to believe the bastards to maintain your sanity. It so happens that the next eight pages of my logbook contain the record of 118 sorties. I always knew that 'They' had no parents.

The first landing at Meiktila was under shell fire. I assume it was the Japs, but since being shot down by the British Army I was never quite sure again. Ghurkas were sitting around honing their kukris. We unloaded the ammo and took off in a cloud of dust with indecent haste. A pilot who landed later saw no Ghurkas. Later that day they were to be seen again, honing their kukris having successfully seen off the opposition. Later that day we landed at Myitche. A landing at Alon followed a supply drop at Kamye. I was glad to be at the wheel, suffering as I do from vertigo. The open door, on my occasional trip to the loo, seemed to draw me towards it. Some pilot! Turning in my seat and circuiting I could see the parachutes on their way down, and the free-falling tyres bounding off into the jungle. Our second sortie on 14th March was our first into Mandalay. What a damn silly song – Mandalay was hundreds of miles from the sea; there were no flying fishes playing anywhere.

As the busy days passed, as CMC of the Sergeants' Mess, I was anxiously following the building of our mess basha. It was being built adjacent to the field kitchen, connected to it by a roofed walkway. The roof was of palm fronds. It was difficult to run a bar from my living quarters, which I shared with Nick, WO Dark and a long-toothed Flight Sergeant store basher. Came the day that the mess was ready, and tables and chairs were installed. All looked forward to the gala opening. The floor was covered with rugs and carpets, the tables all had new sheets for tablecloths, there were glasses and jugs, platters for bread and shining stainless steel cutlery. What luxury. What envy our mess aroused in the zobits! How proud was this Chairman of the Mess Committee. The first meal I don't remember, but it must have hit the right place. Alcoholic beverages flowed and we returned to our bashas after dinner. Within a few minutes there were shouts of 'FIRE!'. There was our new mess, burning from the covered way end – a petrol stove had gone up. We rushed into the hut, rescuing what chairs and tables and mats that we could lay our hands on. It was hopeless. Sparks were falling as I staggered out behind the last salvageable table. The roof was consumed in seconds and forlornly we watched it burn, until we realised that neighbouring bashas were in danger of going up too. Open for one night only. Far, far worse was to come. Within a few days the CO presented me with a bill for 1200 rupees in respect of sheets, carpets, candlesticks, crockery and so on. The bill came from Bilaspur as had the furnishings. Certain regular SNCOs had purloined it all just prior to our departure to Tulihal. Most had gone up in smoke. My pay was but 90 rupees a week, so I was glad there was no hassle when I asked that each member contribute towards the debt.

A trip to Mandalay North on 25th March nearly solved my impecunious state. A Sikh soldier, honest looking, sold me seven cut diamonds for twelve rupees. Back at base I unwrapped and displayed my treasure. 'You can tell if they are genuine,' said an old soldier. 'Put them between two coins and jump on them.' So persuaded, I did just that. The stones turned to powder. They were paste!

Japs were back in Meiktila, or else it was the weather. We started dropping supplies there from 23rd March. We landed at Ondaw, Myitche, Monywa and Tada-U, dropping at Sagaing and Meiktila, sometimes three sorties, up to ten hours airborne in the day, without the time and energy spent in unloading. We carried everything from toilet rolls to Bailey bridging, and if there were no casualties to bring back there were always the ubiquitous supply chutes which had to be collected for re-use.

At some time in mid-March, enjoying a rest day siesta lying all but naked under the mozzy net, I was no doubt in the land of nod. Suddenly awakened I was surprised to hear running footsteps and curses as semi-naked SNCOs sped by my basha doorway. It was womanly and girlish laughter, unladylike screams too, which added to my surprise. Whether they were all Naga women or not I don't know. Some were brazenly topless. All were painted an ochre red. Why were the boys running? Wouldn't it have been fun to hang around and see? Bravely I struggled with the option for all of a split second. Then I joined the retreat, barefooted but with the whitest of hand towels. We all scattered down various jungle paths, some females in pursuit. Other 'ladies' made for the Canadian lines. There they caught the Canadian Station Warrant Officer in the shower and subjected the struggling gent to certain indignities and fondlings, until he was finally released, covered from the navel down with red ochre. The red ochre, we learned, represented the menstrual fluid of one of their female fertility gods. The Station Warrant Officer appeared to be temporarily impotent. Those of us who by luck or design had escaped the attentions of these dark Amazons eventually found our way back to our bashas. From there we were able to watch our dhobi wallah beat hell out of his red-ochred wife as he drove her back to the village.

The weather was worsening, but up to the 25th March no supply drops had been aborted. My crew had flown over eighty sorties and had accrued 260 operational hours. On 29th March 1944 we flew twice down to Akyab, an airstrip on an island off the coast of Burma. The second trip completed our squadron move, and one of our passengers was a wireless op's pet security guard; a charming little monkey. We set up home yet again. Each crew was now in a tent, and each crew dug its own well, and lined it with topless and bottomless forty-gallon drums. Cool, pure water was but six feet down in the sandy soil. Luxury! Our alcoholic rations were kept at the bottom of these wells. On 7th April, WO Sewell flew my crew back to Tulihall to collect 466 which had been left U/S and undergoing inspection.

Operations went on just the same; three sorties a day into Burma, over the Arakan mountains. The monsoon weather got steadily worse. The first sortie was usually straightforward after a 5 am take off (reveille was at 3.30 am). The clouds didn't start to build up over the mountains until after 9 am. Outward bound on the second sortie required more height, but the return just after midday was dicey. The cumulus built up as one watched, the bulbous, towering clouds visibly expanding and contracting. Clear lanes closed behind the aircraft or, worse still, in front. The Dak plunged and rose, 'George' was no good in this weather – flying was by the wet seat of one's pants. Day after day was the same.

On such a day a Dakota of our sister squadron was deemed lost over the Arakans. The navigator was Sgt. Eden, Anthony Eden's son. We spent a lot of time during our first clear sorties, for many days, searching for signs in the jungle. We found nothing. I do not believe that authorities have found anything since, so that the jungle must be very unexplored or the aircraft went down in the sea. Thereafter his squadron began to lose quite a number of aircraft, almost all to the weather. I believe that our European winter experience, plus squadron training policy, gave us the edge and until then we had lost no one. Luck did play its part.

On one occasion, returning empty from a drop, we sailed into a fissure between the clouds at about 7500 feet, over the Arakans. After a twisting passage the fissure closed on us, involving a steep climbing turn into the cloud. What a gigantic thump! All instruments went haywire, so that any struggle with the controls was speculative. All sense of altitude and direction was lost. Buffeted by abnormal pressures the crew needed little urging to don their 'chutes. I'll give Nick his due, he did return from the fuselage to proffer me my 'chute. As I reached out to take it we were all amazed to find ourselves hurled out of the top of the cloud into the sunshine, almost on an even keel. The instruments settled and told part of the story. My prayers were answered. George and Dick were still on board. I feared that they might have jumped, though what would have happened I shudder to think – they would have gone straight up. In what could have been no more than thirty seconds we had been hurled out of that towering cumulus at 12,500 feet. A mile, straight up, in a few seconds. Orientated, it was child's play to find base. Shattered nerves were not calmed by a couple of bacon sandwiches. It took two days on whisky and Easton's syrup to regain one's moral fibre.

Gambling took place on most evenings in the mess, and a co-pilot with a broken leg was always in on the scene. There was no trouble despite the stakes, and discipline was good. Then Kitty sent me a Monopoly set which, after a while, I placed in the mess 'lounge bar'. It was incredible to believe that such a harmless parlour game, with make-believe money, could cause so many arguments and fights. Monopoly took the place of poker and the boys played the game long after 2300 hours when I was duty bound to close the mess. After several late and rowdy nights, and several reprimands from Wg. Cdr. Hillary, our new CO, I resorted to pulling out the fuses in the mess at 2315 hours. On the first evening that this was necessary several drunks sought me out at my basha for revenge. Foolishly I got up, hopped out of the rear window and carried out a flanking movement. Still in pyjamas I crept up behind them. My shouted orders from the rear had the required effect, thank goodness, and they dispersed. On the day following I found that all the spirit measures had disappeared from the bar, together, I suspect, with some navy gin. I therefore closed the bar for two nights, and was never more unpopular.

In this Theatre the airmen had four half-pint bottles of beer a month, the SNCOs had the four bottles of beer and a bottle of spirits, whilst the zobits had two bottles of spirits. We SNCOs were able to supplement our rations with two-gallon casks of Indian navy gin and rum, so we willingly gave our four bottles of beer to the airmen who worked long hours to service the kites. I would have liked to have instigated the programme of parties which I well remember taking place monthly, with the ground staff on 70 Squadron, in the desert. However we really did work so hard that a whole day was necessary to recuperate from the three sorties we undertook. For my part I rarely drank other than at the end of a flying day. Then it was glorious charp. There was always the dhobi and writing home to do, as well as re-digging drainage ditches to keep the surroundings dry. We did not have a particular aircraft, but flew whichever was available and loaded. On most occasions we finished the day out with the aircraft with which we started at 0500 hours.

With the advent of the monsoons it was noticeable that the warrant officer skippers who made up one third of the crews were carrying out two-thirds of the work load. Sqn. Ldr. R.A. Browne, 'A' Flight Commander, confirmed my suspicions, and confided that the CO was not unaware of the fact. The morale of the SNCO crews was high, and we were compensated by the numberless delicious bacon sandwiches which we consumed between sorties.

During April I was to learn that my school pal, Eddie Knowles, a flying officer pilot, had been killed on the Rhine do. He had been converted, due to a surplus of pilots, first to stoking railway engines, and then to flying Horsa gliders. His son was but a few weeks old, and I had only the month before received a letter describing his frantic search for a pram and a cot. I had met his wife once, before they were married, in Leamington Spa, where the Home Office had been moved. His letters were always amusing, self-deprecating. He was a very good friend, as were his parents and his sister. His glider received a direct hit prior to landing. The European war was coming to an end and Eddie, a good, quiet fellow, had bought it. Who makes the selection? And why? However distant the tragedy, morale flagged and I was once more lacking in moral fibre. I quickly recovered with the help of the Doc and liberal quantities of the bitter pick-me-up called Easton's syrup which, the quack said, contained strychnine glycerophosphate. The glider pilots had been threatened with Lack of Moral Fibre Boards to ensure the 'volunteering'.

On through April went the landings and drops, still three a day, every other day. To Tatkon, Lewe, Tennent, Myin-

187

gyan, Kalawya, Pyingbongyi, Natmauk and Taungdwingyi. On one occasion we were hurled out of the door of our plane by a huge charge of static electricity. The refuelling airman was thrown off the wing. We had landed on a newfangled bitumenised canvas airstrip, and the trailing earthwire had failed to operate through the insulated ground cover. The wire was poked through the bitumen and the kite was discharged completely. On 3rd May an op to Rangoon was aborted. An engine cut just as we had over-flown the Arakans, and was restarted by judiciously holding down the starter priming switch.

On the 5th we set off in a different kite to take petrol near Rangoon. With the Arakans safely behind us we were stooging quietly over mangrove and jungle at two thousand feet when there was a tack-tack-tack from the hydraulic relief valve. Now the cure was to momentarily operate the undercarriage lever and relieve the pressure build-up. Nicky did so, knowing the drill, but the tack-tack-tack didn't stop. Looking up and out I espied tracers whipping by the nose of the Dak. A machine gun was firing from a clearing below and we had been flying through the slipstream of the tracers. Much too close. The Japs must have overestimated our speed. We circled out of range and called up the Beaufighters. The Japs below had obviously been outflanked. We didn't hang around, but heard they were properly dealt with. We had contemplated dropping forty gallons of petrol on them in one lump, but thought better of it. The petrol would be better used elsewhere. It dawned on us afterwards that a hit with one of those tracers would have caused a bonfire in the sky. We carried almost seven hundred gallons in forty-gallon drums.

On 6th May 1945, in Dakota KN 400 our newest addition, we flew Group Captain Grandy to Rangoon together with Flight Lieutenant Sinclair. The Japs had evacuated Rangoon and a welcome was painted on Rangoon prison roof by the inmates. We landed at Mingladon after an uneventful trip and unloaded our medical orderlies, their supplies and our cargo. We picked up eight ex POWs, seven of whom were stretcher cases, and five other passengers. The leader of the POWs was the only one standing like a ramrod and just as skinny. He was the regimental sergeant major of a Scottish regiment. He stood all the way back to base. These men were the first to be flown out of Rangoon, and were referred to by Marshall of the Royal Air Force Grandy, Chief of Defence Staff, now the Sheriff of Windsor Castle (or Warden – I forget). He was an ex Battle of Britain pilot, but did not want to fly my Dak. As a direct consequence of that trip my CO was instructed by the group captain to recommend me for a commission. Somehow I always have the habit of speaking the truth, when diplomacy would pay, and it was the group captain himself who turned me down at interview. He it was who had to approve my gong, however.

Those eight POWs were flown to Shillong, up in the hills near Darjeeling, to recuperate. After three weeks they were flown home but were killed in a flying accident when crossing the French Alps, just an hour or two from home. WHY? After years in Japanese hands it was a cruel cut.

One landing was made at Myingyan, and two drops at Kalawya and Pegu on 9th May. It was outwards on the second sortie that I think 'it' happened. We were, as was our wont, listening in with one ear to the BBC Forces Overseas programme. THE WAR IN EUROPE WAS OVER, VE DAY was announced! Elation there was, but slightly tempered. What the hell was I doing here, Churchill? That news caused the rest of the day to drag inconsequentially. Back at base preparations for a party were in full swing. Our Anglo-Indian teetotal adjutant was organising the sale of hooch from unknown sources. Tea urns were placed on trestle tables and all the alcohol we could find was poured willy nilly into them. Those not full were topped up with squash and a little de-icer fluid. The brews were very mixed and very, very different, but there was not time to select. The party had started. Enamel mugs were filled, they held one pint, and airmen, SNCOs and zobits were soon paralytic, later unconscious. The adjutant was counting his money. Had the Japanese had an able-bodied man within a mile or two we must all have been annihilated. A penknife would have done it. One of us nearly was a goner. He fell headfirst down a well, turned around inside the forty-gallon drum, and stood in the cool water for hours, calling for help and polluting it.

A mention of the adjutant reminds me that he had the brain of a merchant. One day I flew bags of old worn KD into an airstrip where the old clothing was swapped for a cow and one hundred and fifty chickens. On the return trip the cow was a dirty incontinent passenger and the chickens all died, whether from lack of air or fright at high flying I don't know. The adj. tethered the cow outside the orderly room and milked it daily. We ate the chickens, but it cost us!

I think it was on 14th May that we all transferred to Akyab Main aerodrome, just outside the town. There was no accommodation for us so we had to erect our tents in a coconut grove which was prone to flooding. We therefore cut down enough coconut trees to form a twelve-foot square with the trunks two high. We filled the square with earth and sand, and our ridge rent had a plinth high enough to keep us out of the floods. We found, later, that the coconut grove owner had to be compensated with 100 rupees for every tree so destroyed. I wondered if the adj. was in on that. At any rate a mess was erected and we dug the latrines. Showers were engineered from forty-gallon drums on trestles. Water was, at most, less than a foot below the surface, so that latrines were full before we used them. They were soon full of maggots too, so that bottoms were not far above the pollution. Needless to say we didn't dig wells here. Drops and landings followed the same pattern and operational hours mounted. Four hundred and eighty two hours in total by the end of May. One hundred and fifty nine sorties. Hang on Blighty, be with you soon.

By this time all fripperies had been lost and the mess was a plain unadorned basha. The armourers supplemented our rations by stunning sea fish with cordite. Frequently, in splashing along to the mess, members floundered in newly dug but flooded drainage ditches. We did our own dhobi. Leisure time was normally spent doing chores, writing home or kipping. I still stand to be corrected, but I believe that no other pilots anywhere had ever flown so many hours a month in such vile, in fact in any, weather. We were almost exhausted, certainly anxious. Flying hours per month had increased considerably. December, 55 hours; January, 49 hours; February, 44 hours 30 minutes; March, 89 hours; April, 107 hours; May, 106 hours 35 minutes. 'George' was useless in such weather. Flying was by the seat of one's pants. What would June and July bring? Well June was to be a rest. Only 86 hours at the controls and another course of Easton's syrup! Since many of us were getting very near to tour-expired, the powers counted any amount of landings between take-off and return to base as one sortie. Cynically we saw the 'tour-ex' target recede into the distance. Lots of new names in the log were proof of the army's advance. Payegyi, Madauk, Tabaugi, Kalawya, Pegu, Zwataung, Toungoo and Thirrawaddy. On one of the foulest days we were forced to ask for a QDM from Meiktila. Over strange mountains after half an hour we realised we had been given a reciprocal, and were many miles east. At least that was what the newfangled radio altimeter seemed to be telling us.

At about 1500 hours on one rest day early in May, having

just showered, I was about to dry off and get charp-borne when Ronnie Drew shouted from the mess that the CMC was wanted on the phone most urgently. More trouble, or was it my ticket at last? Still drying indecently I picked up the phone and almost dropped it in surprise. I'm sure I instinctively covered up. 'Would the CMC and three other Squadron members like to come to dinner tonight?' said an unexpected female voice. It was a nursing sister from the local military hospital which had just been manned with some ladies. (Manned seems the correct term, but what would one say today?) With some qualms, quite unused to female company, we set off down the muddy track for my one and only visit to the 'town'. I didn't feel like a young man of twenty-two going on his first date for three and a half years. What would be expected of us? Eventually we arrived at a wooden hut built on stilts, and on the verandah we were met by a big lovely girl, our hostess. The reader is waiting for her name – I'm ashamed, I can't remember. Hope she reads this. There were three others but I cannot describe one of them, due solely to the hurricane lamplight. The meal was good, considering the environs and the NAAFI rations. It was very romantic but my unease increased with my ignorance as to how I should handle this situation. I liked the nursing sister who was so thoughtful and hospitable, but somehow I felt that I didn't want to pursue the contact. I felt strangely caddish, yet relieved when we left. It was late and at 0330 hours we were to start another flying day. This very civilising meeting lifted our morale for days, whilst our mess-mates pumped us for gen, and would not believe our protests of complete celibacy.

In May, too, George Telford my W/Op. for almost a year was suddenly repatriated to Newcastle where his mother was critically ill. The tears in my eyes at our parting were for me, not for him! Then a further calamity in the same month. Dick Sheppard, my navigator, was asked by another new skipper to crew for him. This new chap had been Dick's skipper at OTU and he had pressed Dick. It didn't do much for my ego, or my morale, and it left Nicky and I more than a little worried. I think Flt. Sgt. Holt or Sgt. Collier took over from George. A Flt. Sgt. Weekes also flew with me sometimes. I was landed with a spare navigator from the Officers' Mess, a Flying Officer Dusty Miller. He was more rusty than dusty, as he had not kept abreast of the navigator aids available.

Somehow we survived without memorable incident until our one hundred and seventy sixth operation on the 17th June 1945. Things always happened to me on birthdays and on anniversaries. 17th June 1940 was the day I started work at Allen West and here, five years later to the day, I was to come close to meeting my Waterloo. Dusty had turned up that morning as usual, with his green navigator's bag containing his pencil, rule, piece of string and silk escape map (I still have mine). Our hope, or fear, was that we should complete two or three sorties that day, but it was not to be. The flight and landing at Toungoo were reasonably uneventful but on the return we noted in awe a massive build-up of cloud which covered the Arakans and had spread over the Burmese plains. We were soon in ten-tenths cloud and feeling our way homewards at one thousand feet above the highest expected mountain on our track. On and on we droned and bounced, scared absolutely witless. I told Dusty to get Akyab Beacon on the Eureka box as we rode the storm. Only Eureka might show us our position and, what seemed hours later, Dusty said, 'You can let down now.' What a relief! Slowly we descended, peering through the pea soup for a gap.

What a shock awaited Nicky and me as we strained our eyes. The tops of trees hove into view only feet below us, and we were still at over three thousand feet! Throttles opened wide, pitch fully fine, mixture in rich, blower engaged and stick pulled back. Then eyes shut and a desperate prayer. We roared back into the thickest cloud. What could we do if a mountain loomed ahead? No Dak has responded or climbed quicker. To hell with the cu-nimbs, the mountains seemed harder at that juncture! At what height we levelled out I don't remember. Plenty high enough. Pants were wringing wet. Still in cloud. Dusty corrected my course and twenty minutes later came the words, 'Now you can let down, Skipper.' No way; no bloody way Dusty. 'I will fly on till I am directly over the Eureka beacon, whose position I know.' I had never been so shaken and I insisted that the whole crew confirm the picture on the tube as we overflew the beacon. That done, still very high, I circled, losing height. Buffeted in rain storms we descended to one thousand feet where we caught a fleeting glimpse of a shoreline. Now Akyab, at least, was a flattish area so down to five hundred, four hundred, three hundred feet. Suddenly there was the runway but it wasn't Akyab! We were more than fifty miles out. It could only be Ramree, the base of another Dak squadron.

After several attempts we flew along the line of the runway at two hundred feet, and made our usual but much lower circuit. Wheels and flaps down, peering ahead, we flew through the heaviest of monsoon rains and lost sight of the airfield. Sometime we lost the sea too. The final approach leg was the most dicey. Slowly we let down and suddenly saw the runway a little to the right. A swift turn, throttles closed and we were heading for a narrow strip of metalled runway. I should have gone round again but I was desperate. With the weather so foul I thought I might lose sight of the island altogether. In a few seconds we were holding off, the starboard wing just missed the control tower, and the port flashed over the fire tender. DOWN, brakes locked hard on, wheels in a skid on the steel runway, and tail cocked like a scorpion, we slithered along what we now knew to be a narrow taxi track. Thanking God that it was clear, we slid off the end of the track, at a few knots, into the mangrove. The wheels were part buried but the kite appeared undamaged.

I have never laid into a zobit as I did then. Luckily it was only verbally and all witnesses were SNCOs. Dusty had tuned into the wrong Eureka beacon, and he had not recognised the flashing code. Perhaps he had not known of the existence of any other. Tuned into Ramree the signalled distance was at least fifty miles less than that from Akyab. Hence we had let down over the mountains far too soon. High headwinds had not helped. When fifty miles from Akyab the worst of the Arakans had been overflown, but fifty miles from Ramree drops you right in them! That was the one and only time that I ever saw trees in a cloud. Lucky we saw no angels. We were hauled out of the mud, told that the theatre was grounded, had a meal, then in the drier evening we set course for Akyab, flying over the sea all the way. 'Dusty' Miller went back to the mess and Flt. Lt. Coughlan, Sqn. Ldr. Brown's successor, gave me another navigator. I don't recall who Dusty's successor was, but I was shattered, and again on Easton's syrup. Another dozen ops were completed in the remaining thirteen days of June.

I thanked God that the new CO, Wg. Cdr. Walter Hillary, took my flight commander's advice and sent us all off to Shillong, a rest camp near Darjeeling, way up in the hills where the rainfall was less than Akyab, a mere two hundred inches per year. Correction; two hundred inches in the five-month monsoon period. I have not recorded our flight as passengers to Sylhet, and I remember little of it, a schedule via Calcutta. However at Sylhet we were directed to a Chevrolet three-ton truck driven by a Sikh soldier. Apparently much of the road into the highlands was single track. Every two hours or so the direction of the traffic changed. It was soon obvious why. From my seat near the tail-board

my eyes were continually drawn to the chasms and preci-
pices which slid by at great speed, as the driver wound his
way up the mountain road. Dear God guide that Sikh's
hands, I prayed; ensure that no broken-down vehicle
remains on the road, either in a tunnel or round a hairpin
bend; let there be no landslide and please ensure that the
tyres remain fully inflated. It was a hair-raising trip and I
dreaded for the whole of the next fourteen days our trip
back. The Chevy could do sixty uphill! Please God give us
a driver whose chief concern was living. Unhappily it was
too far to walk. Arrive we did, if somewhat shattered, and
the whole truckload were put through a rigorous FFI. The
inspection was carried out by a Flt. Sgt. medical orderly
who knew the temptations of the Khasi girls who lived in
huts in the valley, and also knew that they gave doses away
with their favours. What steely suspicious eyes he had; he
must have thought that we had come from the fleshpots of
Delhi. Wonder where those Khasi girls got the VD in the
first place. From the permanent staff at Shillong? Or the
pre-war Pukka-sahib tea planters? We were suitably warned
and impressed and none of my crew wandered valley-wards.

I spent the whole fourteen days, my first leave since
Habbaniya days in 1943, resting, eating and sleeping in for
as long as I could. We were well entertained. I danced with
the delightful protégée of the local district commissioner.
Her conversations dwelt on such places as Southampton,
London and Edinburgh. I was quite homesick. Later I
learned that she was Anglo-Indian and had never even left
India. She obviously read about England avidly against the
day that she might have her dreams fulfilled. The Diplomatic Corps did their best to entertain us. We enjoyed the
impromptu competition between two trumpet players, one
an American from a well-known 'Big Band', and the other
a South African who played with the London Philharmonic.
The latter played the Trumpet Voluntary more sweetly than

I have heard it either before or since. Most of us had tears running down our cheeks. The pair of them had identical applause, so that the competition was deemed a draw.

On several evenings we indulged in fried egg swallowing competitions. The rules were strict. No egg was to be bitten, and there was to be the minimum of delay between swallows. I won the final, after a run-up of probably one hundred eggs, against a sailor of the Royal Navy. I managed sixteen whole fried eggs on that occasion, and had four eggs and chips for supper soon afterwards. It was a good job that the Indian chicken-fruit is somewhat smaller than its European counterpart. I must say that such puerile behaviour confirmed a complete lack of officer qualities. Just a novel form of the Schooner race, and I've been forced into taking part in many of those, invariably losing, against the officers.

At a goldsmith's in Shillong bazaar I bought Kitty a gold bracelet with quite a few milky opals set in it, and a pair of matching earrings. The perpetual rain didn't seem to bother us. We were charpborne and chairborne, and our feet were grounded. The leave sped by and my nerves better stood the descent into Sylhet on 18th July. We flew back to Akyab via Calcutta where we night-stopped at Dum-Dum and I bought an opal ring which almost matched the bracelet. Collectively we bought crates of eggs in the market to take back to the mess. We dispensed charity liberally to those who told us the story, to crippled kids and to single, extremely young mothers with fly-covered babies, and flew back to Akyab the next day. The mess was delighted to receive the several gross of eggs, packed in straw in bamboo crates. Most of the benefit we had reaped from our leave was to dissipate with the news that Warrant Officer Walton and his crew had been lost in the sea just outside Akyab harbour, during a severe, visibility-curtailing rainstorm. I believe that a wing tip had dipped in. He was a good fellow and a personal friend, not one to shirk his duty whatever the detail. His navigator was the most Christian Christian that I had met before or since. A bulwark of our bamboo church. Why them? Then and now I've often sought the answer. Then as now I cannot find it. The devil must win many of the battles.

A New Zealand warrant officer and his crew were also missing, but rumours were rife that some or all of the crew might be recovered. They had been overloaded with Bailey-bridging girders and had gone down into the jungle on one engine. That damn Bailey bridging was just too heavy for three crew to jettison. That was the one cargo I hated. In a forced landing it was likely to come through the bulkheads anyway. Rumours were correct. Although I never saw the Kiwi or his crew again (he lived in the next tent to me – can't remember his name) we learned that they had been very lucky to find some sort of rocky clearing in which to flop. Somehow, stripped of wings, they had survived deep in the jungle. All but one were uninjured. I believe it was the navigator who injured his spine and broke a limb. The crew carried him until they met a stream; they followed the stream and came across a small hut. One member stayed with the injured man and the other two marched for two days down jungle paths following the stream. They met some friendly natives who took them to a white-haired English forester who had spent his war in the jungle. Somehow he had avoided or evaded the Japs. He immediately recognised the hut from the Kiwi's description and all were soon rescued. The injured man and his guardian were reported to extol the virtues of cooked, then latterly uncooked, lizards which kept them supplied with protein. Try as I may I cannot bring that skipper's name to mind. It may have been Gulliver. A contemporary of his was a WO F.H. Moffat from Invergowrie, NSW, who would know more of the story.

Between 20th and 31st July 1945 we flew ten more sorties.

My total, including the thirty-seven bombing raids, became 234. Almost 900 of my 2100 hours were operational. Over 300 hours had been night flying. I'm sure that that total was beaten, but not by many. It represented an average of thirty-nine hours for each month since my first air experience on Tiger Moths.

There was little wonder then that, with Nicky my co-pilot, I was delirious to find that I was to be part of a 267 Squadron detachment destined to operate from Delhi and Karachi. I didn't have to clear the squadron for a detachment, and on 3rd August 1945 I said my farewells and flew with Nicky, Plt. Off. Webb and Plt. Off. Edwards to Mauripur via Maharajpur. Flt. Lt. Kopperud was the detachment commander, a large blond South African. I believe we were three aircraft and crews.

No sooner had we arrived in Karachi than I chose to have the quacks investigate the reasons for my now frequent high temperature. In Mauripur Hospital I enjoyed ten days under observation. Enjoyed? Well not quite. Subjected twice daily to blood tests I dreaded the WAAF orderly who stabbed at my thumb with her eyes shut, so I mustered my courage and took over the job myself. Then there was another lass who was more professional, but she placed the needle where she wanted and deliberately pushed. In conversation I discovered that she had been a girl groom at the stables in Seaford next door to my father's garage business. (I recall now another coincidence when I received a parcel of comforts from the WVS. It came from a lady in East Street, Seaford and contained a balaclava and a pullover. The only trouble was that I was in Iraq at the time, and the temperature was 125 degrees Fahrenheit in the shade!)

At the end of ten days, good nursing had normalised me and I was due for discharge on the morrow. Nothing had been found to be wrong. However when the Doc came round to give me my ticket, he ordered me back into bed, sharp. Without a word he passed me a mirror, and I beheld a very yellow visage therein. I had caught jaundice from patients in nearby beds. By the next morning I was really ill. Couldn't keep anything down, even water came up. This went on for another two weeks, when my normal unhealthy pallor returned. I watched a sick army warrant officer being visited by his family, an Indian wife and a few little children. It appeared that he had been in India by choice for ten years and was now being forcibly evacuated to Blighty, alone. Whether the family were to follow I don't know, but the tears portrayed the wife's fears for the future.

In August, whilst in hospital, I learned of the atom bombs dropped on Hiroshima and Nagasaki. There seemed nothing remotely immoral about such attacks which, with VJ day on 15th August must have saved many, many thousands of allied lives, both prisoners and combatants. It was all over. I had made my last flight in anger, unless the Russkis intervened somewhere. To all of us this was a very real possibility. There was no party, only a very deep and thankful sense of utter relief.

Out of hospital I flew my first flight in peacetime, a trip to Jiwani on 16th September, my brother's birthday. The following day I was to say goodbye to the detachment who returned without me to Mingladon, Rangoon, where 267 Squadron now operated. Somehow my state of health, and the fact that I would be four years tour-ex in six weeks, raised some compassion somewhere. I was left behind in the transit camp at Mauripur to await my airlift to Blighty. Left behind with me, but in much more comfort, was the detachment flight commander, Flt. Lt. Kopperud. He was due for repatriation to South Africa. At that stage he certified the totals in my flying log, and, at my prompting, he decided that as a transport pilot I must be above average. Maybe a bit more pressure would have squeezed out an 'Exceptional' assessment! The food in the transit camp, where there was a multitude of servicemen to feed, was atrocious – often excellent food spoiled, but most often bad food before it was processed. Hours were wasted on the bogs as a result of eating it. Eventually the caterers gave up the impossible task and thousands of American 'K' ration packs were placed just inside the front door of the mess. A breakfast, lunch or dinner pack could be selected without one being assaulted by the vile smell that pervaded the place. Most, if not all, withdrew to their tents with the required concentrated rations. The breakfast pack was popular because of the four sheets of real toilet paper, the three Chesterfield cigarettes and the hard tack and marmalade. Lunch contained a small tin of cheese, hard tack, boiled sweets, three cigarettes and no toilet paper, whilst dinner was all edible. Some sort of Spam, malted milk tablets, boiled sweets, a solid block of soup. We always gave away the hard block of oatmeal in the breakfast ration since it needed prolonged soaking and we had no means of heating it. I am sure it would have been better suited to a ship's repair kit – an excellent caulker.

I was getting my mail regularly and quickly now. Kitty had arranged for the banns to be read and for our wedding to be a double one with her younger sister, who was marrying a Canadian. This was to be on 3rd November, just two days before my four years were up. Of course I would be home by then. One morning I received a letter addressed to Sergeant Barfoot, which had been posted in India, but had travelled far. Quite a puzzle. It was not uncommon for a letter to take a year to catch up if postings had intervened, but I had been a warrant officer for all of two years. Opening it I was amazed to find that it was meant for other eyes, albeit those of a clansman. 'Dear ----------, we had such a glorious time during your last leave and I hope we can repeat it soon. My husband leaves for the hills shortly so that if . . . etc. etc.' It appeared to be a letter from a nurse in a Calcutta hospital, but it was obvious that the intended recipient must have missed his assignation. My worry was, what if such a letter arrived on the doormat in England, having followed me home? Eventually I took the letter to the camp adjutant and explained my predicament. Did he leer disbelievingly? He agreed to write to the girl to tell her that her letters were getting into the wrong hands. Some many years later I was to meet that 'Sgt.' Barfoot and it disturbed him greatly. At any rate I acquired evidence of my innocence, should it ever be required.

Here at Mauripur I was sought out by WO Lee Randall, 'Candy', an old school friend. He had spent some months behind German lines in Holland, hidden on a barge and well looked after by a Dutch family. His Tempest had been shot down. Now he was on his way to some unsuspecting Dak squadron as second pilot. Was I glad to be going the other way? Well, I thought I was. Candy told me of the excitement that was going on at home. I didn't stand a dog's chance he said, and advised me to stay where I was. I would be straight off the plane and up the church steps, he said. There were still five weeks to go. Would I make it in time? Time passed slowly. I was sure that I had been forgotten so made frequent trips to the Air Transport Wing at Drigh Road.

Flt. Lt. Kopperud and I hit it off, and we shopped, visited and ate together at the local Chinese restaurants. We selected Indian rugs to be packed and shipped home. I selected a blue and beige one, 7ft by 3ft, costing 110 rupees. We saw them later, packed in hessian and ready for shipment.

After a while 'Kopper' decided that we could enjoy our enforced wait if he made me an officer, so, with KD crisp and starched, and wearing my officer-type glengarry, I wore two of his badges of rank on my epaulettes, and we started to enjoy the fleshpots of the Officers' Club together. I was very apprehensive indeed. Discovery would mean demotion perhaps. But day after day we swam in the club pool, and ate in the club dining room. I became more worried as we came to be accepted by other frequent visitors, especially the nurses who could have recognised me from my long stay at the hospital. Then calamity! I lost one of the two ringed epaulettes. Kopper merely cut the remaining one in half and I entered the Officers' Club under the enquiring gaze of the Indian manager, as a flying officer. Demoted overnight! I never went back, as I believed that wheels were in motion for my apprehension. Luckily Kopper soon left for South Africa and I fretted my time away.

My wedding day came at last, and where was I? Still at Mauripur. Kitty must have wondered whether I was coming back at all. Her younger sister had beaten her to it after a very short engagement. It was now four and a half years since Kitty had accepted my proposal. On 4th November I was informed that I was to fly out on the morrow, exactly four years to the day since I had left Hampstead Norris in Berkshire with the Wingco. They took their pound of flesh. I raced around trying to get paid, without luck, trying to hand in my trusty forty-five, without luck, and catching up on my jabs. Came the Fifth of November, a memorable day, and a strange aircraft was waiting to take me home. It looked like a dragonfly on very long front legs. It was a Stirling, whose reliability could not be trusted. I weighed my baggage under the avaricious eye of a movements sergeant. Too heavy! Reduce your baggage by ten pounds. Defiance was useless and I had to part with my white rollneck aircrew sweater, the one I had worn in a Bari pantomime, together with a thin all-wool American blanket. By strapping on my forty-five, wrapping two thin blankets round my middle, and wearing my scruffy, dusty greatcoat over all, I got away with it. My own weight had soared with the reduction in my baggage and I staggered to the Stirling.

203

I don't recall and I didn't record that flight. At least it was pointing the right way.

There was no delay and off we flew, making Lydda Airport on 6th November. All sorts of thoughts, longings and apprehensions fill one's mind after such a long absence. The daily mepacrine and the jaundice had left me looking like a half chat Jap. Under my padding I was skinny. I had plenty of time to worry since at Lydda there was a backlog for Blighty. The nights of 6th, 7th and 8th November went by and I had no way to tell Kitty where I was. Each day we gathered news and rumours at the bogs. Now Lydda was the only place I know where the bogs were a communal eighteen-seater, where we sat in full view of each other, facing outwards in a large circle, twenty degrees per seat, all held up by a centre pole from the cavern below. The few toilet rolls were passed hand to hand and the air was pungent with lime, *inter alia*.

Eventually my turn came and I was detailed as i/c passengers as we were loaded into the bomb bay of a Liberator. What the hell, we were going home weren't we? It was draughty and uncomfortable but we overflew some of the desert airfields and made Tripoli that same day. Acres and acres of aircraft of all kinds littered the desert airfields. Two were absolutely filled nose to tail, and wing tip to wing tip with the good old Wimpeys. Whatever happened to them? I guess many a palm saw profit before the whole lot were disposed of. How? As scrap? To foreign powers? Literally thousands disappeared, as did phalanxes of tanks, trucks and guns.

At Tripoli we wondered if we would be offloaded again. After all it was a transit camp. But no, the pilot and crew were anxious to get home, having been overseas a week, and after refuelling and a meal we took off. Most of the passengers seemed to have bought small sheepskin rugs at Castel Benito. Now the weather was bad over France and

204

the pilot took the Lib way above oxygen height, 12,000 feet or so. Had we had oxygen I'm sure the pilot would have gone higher. As it was I have never been so cold for so long, and I had blankets. Some other soldiers and airmen were in KD, clutching their little sheepskin rugs. One intrepid soldier asked me for his tin of boiled sweets, since I had the rations. With my gauntleted hand I passed him a tin, which promptly stuck to his bare hand. He then sat with tin and hand between his legs to thaw out. As we plunged about in the turbulence I was reminded of those poor ex-POWs who bought it so near home.

Finally, though, the weather broke and we saw the English Channel. Our descent began. Everyone warmed up a bit and smiles broke out. We were nearly there. Over Lyneham in Wiltshire the pilot passed the message back. The undercart would not lock down. We would have to stooge around a while using fuel and hoping. There was also a lot of praying. All this way for a belly landing, and we were sitting in the bomb bay, our feet but inches from the outer skin. For an hour we circled and then we went in. The fault I believe was with the undercart indicator lights because the wheels were locked down. I don't remember the quality of the landing, but it was the best one ever. We were down. Now taxi carefully. Unlike the Pope I rolled on the ground instead of kissing it. Finally we were bedded down in a freezing hut at 3 am. I believe it was at Cliffe Peipard.

HOME AND DEMOB

I was awakened by an almighty bang – we were under attack. A look at my astro-watch showed it to be 11 am on the 11th day of the 11th month in the year nineteen hundred and forty-five. The explosion was a maroon which was wont to be fired on just that occasion, prior to the two minutes silence. All observed those two minutes. They had never meant so much. On the second maroon we all wondered how we could possibly have slept so long here in Blighty.

That afternoon we airforce bods found ourselves on the way by train to a camp near Bassingbourne, where we arrived after dark and hungry. We tramped for miles with our kit and two blankets to a hut, where, without a meal, we turned in. No one welcomed us. On the very next day, 12th November, I was told that I should have gone to Transport Command at Teddington. Loaded like an ox it was back on the train, and it was 1 pm when I arrived at the nearest station to Transport Command. Here I sent Kitty a telegram, 'Meet you at 8 pm Brighton Station'. That was the first she was to know of my safe arrival, and then only second-hand, as her mother phoned her at work at Harringtons in Hove, where she was a draughtswoman.

I left my kit at the station and, still in my khaki battle-dress, found my way to Headquarters. 'No, there is no hope of getting paid and getting a leave pass this day!' Like hell there wasn't! Over four years away from home and only sixty miles from my girl, I was supposed to stay the night? My protestations were heard by a friend in a nearby office who recognised my voice – Warrant Officer Dark, a regular airman pilot, late of 267 Squadron. Here was an ally indeed, and the officious clerks in the orderly room and the accounts departments were given instructions on extracting the digit. If Darkie reads this, then he can be reassured of my everlasting gratitude.

Back on the train and I was patrolling Brighton Station long before 8 pm. Waiting this time was a real pleasure. Almost on the dot I saw Kitty as she came into the station. She was not expecting to meet a 'brown job' but the four years were over in that moment. We sat in a cafe over a cup of tea and let the years roll by. Kitty told me all the news – that, yes, I was nine days late for my wedding. Then she told me that she had been sacked from her job at the drawing office that same afternoon when she asked for, and finally had to demand, leave of absence. She was very indignant since other girls had had frequent leaves and consideration when their boyfriends and husbands had turned up from time to time. I didn't mind, since we would be comfortably off and very happy.

The days before our wedding are hazy, full of planning and catching up. Father and Mother were separated, and the atmosphere difficult except when we were alone. The two Indian rugs arrived; there was no duty to pay. We discovered that the merchant had sent two blue ones, instead of a blue and a beige. There was nothing I could do. The living room would have to be blue also. The stag night on 30th November 1945 was expensive, but I showed myself to Kit, stone sober, before midnight. My best man, younger brother John, was blotto.

The wedding was as I would have had it. My uncle was a bell ringer and a peal of eight was rung for the first time for a wedding since the war. Kitty didn't hear the bells, and I didn't notice her state of undress – a placket was open in her dress at the waist. Her cousin, a naval photographer, clicked away and 125 guests enjoyed a second reception at the Dorothy Café. My father-in-law said, 'You'd better look after her, or else,' and an uncle of mine went missing, to be found much later behind the piano with a bottle of whisky. The photos? The only one to come out was a murky one of the cake. Kit's sailor cousin? Never saw him again. The honeymoon? Father gave me an Austin ten, 1932 vintage, costing all of forty pounds, and we stayed at the White Hart at Fairford, the White Hart at Hereford, and the Royal Hop Pole at Tewkesbury. Kitty had been the tenant of a flat for a few weeks and the world was rosy when we took up residence.

When my leave ended I reported to 187 Squadron at Membury. There Sqn. Ldr. Browne, my erstwhile flight commander of Bari, Tulihall and Akyab, told me that here my experience counted for nought. In the nicest way possible of course. I had to earn some sort of green ticket and, until I did, I wouldn't be allowed to carry a single passenger. The first two weeks in January were spent in checks, cross-country flights and air tests, including a trip to Brussels with WOs Warner, Middleton and Smith as crew. Then came my first scheduled flight for the squadron. On 20th January 1946 I was on my way to bloody India again, with a cargo of penicillin. The round trip took all of twenty days, as we blew a cylinder head when approaching Bahrain. We fretted there for six days, until I persuaded the ground crew that they might use some of the old cylinder head studs again. Apparently this was infra-dig, but it was a good job they did. We might still have been there. We made Mauripur on 29th January and I stormed down to the carpet shop. The merchant saw me coming. His excuse? The rats had eaten the beige rug! I wondered how many times that excuse had been trotted out.

Quite a tour it was. Membury, Elmas, El Adem, Cairo, Habbaniya, Bahrain, Karachi, Masira, Aden, Wadi Halfa, Lydda, El Adem, Catania, Elmas, Istres and Bassingbourne. Then back to Membury after 62 hours in the air for one round trip to Karachi! I got home to find that Kitty was pregnant and anxious that I soon finish my flying days. During that spot of leave I was congratulated by an acquaintance on the award of the Distinguished Flying Cross. He had seen it in the *Argus*. The citation was 'for a very long record of operational flying'. The paper said that I, with a few others, had won the desert war. In *Flight* the list of those gazetted showed that four had been awarded to 267 Squadron members. To WOs Barfoot, Brand and Sewell, and to Flt. Lt. Bramer (whose WAAF intelligence officer acquaintance had once given me her tennis racquet for services rendered. I had given her a lift in my Dak from Rome to Bari). Wg. Cdrs. Francombe and Hillary had both appreciated the efforts of their senior non-commissioned officers. What a coincidence too. The name next to mine in the gazette was WO Gelbauer, the Habbaniya type who had spent some time on the Hurricane rocket squadron in Italy.

On 2nd March it was off again, same destination, different itinerary. Cheesed off, we roared round the Middle East. At Wadi Halfa we stayed the night, attended the ambassador's charity fête and unsportingly won much of his beer on a dartboard game. We were warned off by the lady wife. Arriving back at Membury a few days ahead of schedule I was reprimanded before being posted to 525 Squadron, a sister squadron at the same station.

Four days of captain's checks and GCS approaches followed. On 28th March, on the final approach of a GCS, with hood down, the air traffic controller let me know that my demob had come through. The hood flashed back quickly, despite the examiner's protest. Down on the runway as quickly as possible and out to start clearance from the station and the airforce. No chance. They were applying for my deferment, and I was pushed into the air on the next day for one and a half hours QGH, whatever that was. It was the last flight recorded in my logbooks. The Odyssey of the Ruptured Crab of square-bashing days had come to an end. A grand total of 2283 hours and 25 minutes in five years of flying. Two hundred and thirty four operational sorties.

The great day came and I think I departed for West Drayton for my release. Another coincidence. There before me in the demob queue was WO Micky Gelbauer DFC. Our careers had run almost parallel. We chose a suit, or jacket and trousers, a shirt, a tie, two pairs of socks, a cap or a trilby, and a raincoat. Service braces and underclothes were retained with one kit bag.

We were both to rejoin the colours before five years were up, serving worldwide again. We aided erstwhile enemies and were shot at by former friends. To question reasons and motives was not allowed. Egypt, Aden, Kenya, Oman, Borneo and Indonesia all figure in the post-war story. My last sixteen years of service ended in 1967. They were just as enjoyable, provoking, unfair and exciting.

I have drawn my pension for longer than I had served – fourteen years longer. The lack of officer qualities now bar the state schoolboy from piloting service aircraft. Would another confrontation find enough pilots? I doubt it, but continue to hope that it will never be necessary to find out.